Kent VCs

Kent VCs

Roy Ingleton

Pen & Sword
MILITARY

First published in Great Britain in 2011 by
Pen & Sword Military
an imprint of
Pen & Sword Books Ltd
47 Church Street
Barnsley
South Yorkshire
S70 2AS

ISBN 978-1-84884-409-4

A CIP catalogue record for this book is available from the British Library

Typeset in 11pt Ehrhardt by
Mac Style, Beverley, East Yorkshire

Printed and bound in the UK by
CPI Antony Rowe, Chippenham and Eastbourne

Pen & Sword Books Ltd incorporates the Imprints of Pen & Sword Aviation,
Pen & Sword Family History, Pen & Sword Maritime, Pen & Sword Military,
Pen & Sword Discovery, Wharncliffe Local History, Wharncliffe True Crime,
Wharncliffe Transport, Pen & Sword Select, Pen & Sword Military Classics,
Leo Cooper, The Praetorian Press, Remember When, Seaforth Publishing and
Frontline Publishing.

For a complete list of Pen & Sword titles please contact
PEN & SWORD BOOKS LIMITED
47 Church Street, Barnsley, South Yorkshire, S70 2AS, England
E-mail: enquiries@pen-and-sword.co.uk
Website: www.pen-and-sword.co.uk

Contents

Acknowledgements

It is impossible for me to name all those persons and organizations that have assisted me in my research into the lives, families, deeds and, in many cases, deaths, of the men from Kent who were awarded the Victoria Cross – the ultimate British decoration 'For Valour' – but I would like just to mention the following, in no particular order.

The Burma Star Association; the Centre for Kentish Studies, Maidstone; the Royal West Kent Regiment Archives; Maidstone Museum; Maidstone Library; Medway Archives, Strood; Cranbrook Museum; Dr Adrian Greaves, PhD, MPhil; Andrew Wells; Richard Snow; Tony Grant of the Snodland History Society; and last, but by no means least, the Victoria Cross Society.

There were many more and I trust those that I have not mentioned will forgive me and accept that I appreciate my indebtedness towards them.

To the best of my knowledge and belief, all the text and illustrations used are either in the public domain or, if not, have been included with the permission of the holder(s) of the copyright. If I have inadvertently transgressed in any way I apologize and promise to correct the situation in any future editions.

Roy Ingleton
Maidstone, 22 February 2011

List of Plates

28. Major AM Lafone, VC.
29. Lieutenant Colonel AD Borton, VC.
30. Lieutenant Colonel C Bushell, VC.
31. Lieutenant CH Sewell, VC.
32. Lieutenant DJ Dean, VC.
33. Captain RN Stuart, VC.
34. Lieutenant Commander GS White, VC.
35. HMS E14.
36. Commander CC Dobson, VC.
37. Captain James McCudden, VC.
38. Major E Mannock, VC.
39. Squadron Leader RAM Palmer, VC.
40. A Handley Page Hampden bomber, as flown by Flight Lieutenant RAB Learoyd, VC.
41. Petty Officer TW Gould, VC.
42. Lieutenant Colonel AC Newman, VC.
43. Sergeant TF Durrant, VC.
44. Lieutenant GA Cairns, VC.
45. Lance Corporal JP Harman, VC.
46. Major WP Sidney, VC.
47. Captain LE Queripel, VC.
48. Captain JHC Brunt, VC.
49. Lance Corporal HE Harden, VC.
50. Lieutenant GA Knowlands, VC.

Introduction

I am more ambitious for a reputation for personal courage than for anything else in the world.

(Winston Churchill, 1897)

Although the Ancient Greeks and, later, the Romans had a system of rewarding distinguished service or bravery by badges that soldiers could wear on their clothing, the practice was not adopted in Great Britain until comparatively recently. In the Civil War (1642–1651) some commanders, such as Sir Thomas Fairfax and the Earl of Manchester, issued their own medals but more usually bravery or meritorious service was recognized by a monetary reward or promotion. The system saw a revival in the late eighteenth century when it became fairly common for medals to be issued by societies and individuals, especially regimental commanders. This practice grew during the Napoleonic wars but there was still no official, national recognition available until 1815, when a new military division of the Order of the Bath was instituted. Companionship of that Order (CB) could be granted to junior officers for bravery but was more often than not a reward for distinguished service and devotion to duty.

The originator of the present standardized system of decorations is generally regarded as the Honourable East India Company which in 1837 inaugurated the India Order of Merit, the three classes of which could be conferred on the native Indian troops. However, it took another seventeen years and another major war before the British government was prompted to institute a very limited system of awards for bravery. The Crimean War (1854–1856) was, for the first time, extensively covered by war correspondents such as William Howard Russell of *The Times*, whose stirring tales of courage and valour caught the imagination of the general public back home in Great Britain and created a demand for some form of recognition for these brave men.

Thus spurred into action, the Duke of Newcastle, the Secretary of State for War, wrote to Prince Albert in January 1855 opining that it did not seem right to him 'that such deeds of heroism as the war has produced should go unrewarded by any distinctive outward mark of honour because they are done by privates or officers below the rank of major'. The response came swiftly and only a matter of days later the Duke was able to inform the House of Lords that the government had advised the young Queen Victoria on the creation of three new awards for bravery in the face of the enemy: the Distinguished Conduct Medal (DCM) for the 'other ranks' of the Army; the Conspicuous Gallantry Medal (CGM) for the other ranks of the Royal Navy and Royal Marines; and, finally, the Victoria Cross (VC) open, exceptionally, to *all* ranks of the Army, Royal Navy and Royal Marines.

Most people nowadays know what a Victoria Cross looks like. Its official description in the Royal Warrant is a bronze Maltese Cross bearing the royal crest of a lion over a crown, above a scroll inscribed 'For Valour'. The wording and design were matters of some discussion and in the end it was Queen Victoria herself who chose both the words and the design. In point of fact, the actual cross shape used is more properly described as a 'cross patté' (from the heraldic French for 'with feet' or 'paws', referring to the spreading ends of the cross).

Each rough-cast Victoria Cross is hand-chased to sharpen the detail and then chemically darkened before being suspended from a dark red ribbon (until 1918 VCs awarded to Royal Navy personnel were suspended from a dark blue ribbon). By tradition, the actual cross is made by Hancocks & Co of London from bronze taken from a Russian cannon captured during the Crimean War, but by 1914 the original source had run out and subsequent medals were cast from metal taken from the cascabels from two Chinese coastal defence cannons. The block used for the VCs was 'lost' in 1942 among the thousands of tons of munitions evacuated from the blitzed Woolwich Arsenal. It was rediscovered the following year at the Central Ordnance Depot at Donnington but for a short time an alloy from another source was used.

The Victoria Cross was instituted by Royal Warrant dated 29 January 1856 and the first awards were announced on 24 February 1857. The Royal Warrant stipulated that the VC should only be awarded in wartime and to officers and men who, in the presence of the enemy, 'have then performed some single act of valour or devotion to their country'. It went on to ordain that 'neither rank, nor long service, nor wounds, nor any other circumstance or condition whatsoever, save the merit of conspicuous bravery, shall be held to establish a sufficient claim to the honour'. This rule was amended in a new Royal Warrant signed in 1920 that simply provided that 'the cross shall only be awarded for most conspicuous bravery, or some daring or pre-eminent act of valour or self-sacrifice or extreme devotion to duty in the presence of the enemy'. It was in the same year that the Royal Warrant was officially amended to allow the award of the Victoria Cross posthumously, although in fact posthumous awards had been made in the first decade of the century and during the First World War.

The original Royal Warrant was made retrospective to June 1854 to cover the recently terminated war against Russia. There were 111 Victoria Crosses awarded for bravery during the Crimean War, and details of those granted to officers and men with a Kentish connection will be found in the pages that follow.

The first presentation ceremony occurred in Hyde Park on 26 June 1857 when Queen Victoria, curiously mounted on her horse throughout, pinned VCs on the breasts of sixty-two veterans of the Crimea, the Baltic and the Sea of Azoff. It has remained the custom, wherever possible, that the Victoria Cross should be presented by the monarch in person.

Originally, the order and manner in which medals should be worn was not laid down and they were worn in a variety of ways. It was not until 1881 that Queen's Regulations specified the position of the Victoria Cross when worn with other awards and it was in 1902 that the King directed that the VC was to take precedence over all other medals and decorations.

What is not generally known is the fact that, in order to recognize the bravery of a larger group of men, a VC may be allocated to one representative, elected by a ballot of the man's peers. Indeed, greatly moved by the bravery of all who took part in the disastrous charge of the Light Brigade on 25 October 1854, Prince Albert wrote a memo on 22 January 1855 in which he made the point:

> How is a distinction to be made, for instance, between the individual services of the 200 survivors of Ld Cardigan's Charge? If you reward them all it becomes merely a Medal for Balaclava, to which the Heavy Brigade and the 93rd have equal claims ... [I suggest] that, in cases of general action, it [the VC] be given in certain quantities to particular Regiments, so many to the Officers, so many to the sergeants, so many to the men (of the last, say one per Company) and that their distribution be left to a jury of the same rank as the person to be rewarded ... The limitation of the Numbers to be given to a Regmt at one time enforces the necessity of a selection and diminishes the pain to those who cannot be included.

Forty-six awards have been made in this way. In the case of the Light Brigade, the following names were submitted:

Private Parkes, 4th Light Dragoons
Lance Sergeant Malone, 13th Light Dragoons
Sergeant Berryman, 17th Lancers
Sergeant Wooden, 17th Lancers
Lieutenant Dunn, 11th Hussars

There was no candidate from the 8th Hussars, possibly because of the illness and death of the commanding officer of the regiment at the critical time. One of the above five holders of the Victoria Cross, Sergeant Wooden, had close Kent connections and his story is told later in this book.

The final instruction in the original Royal Warrant specified that any holder of the VC who was subsequently convicted of 'treason, cowardice, felony or of any infamous crime' should have his name erased from the register and forfeit his special pension. It was not clear whether he should in fact surrender the actual decoration. In the period between 1863 and 1908, eight men had their VCs cancelled for some reason or another (most probably the committing of a felony, which could be an act as trifling as a simple theft) and were required to surrender their medal, but this practice was abolished in 1908. In 1920 George V made it very clear that, no matter the crime committed by anyone on whom the VC has been conferred, the decoration should not be forfeited. 'Even were a VC sentenced to be hanged for murder, he should be allowed to wear his VC on the scaffold.' Happily, such a situation has never arisen and no VC has been withdrawn since 1908.

The degree of bravery exhibited during a particular action is always difficult to determine. Were the actions of Private X more courageous than those Sergeant Y or Captain Z in other incidents? Was the action a selfless case of bravery or perhaps more a matter of self-preservation? We now have a wide range of decorations available, depending on the perceived level of courage, and it seems clear that the degree of gallantry required to merit the more prestigious decorations is now much higher than was the case when the Victoria Cross was first instituted. Some of the very early actions which earned a VC would only have been seen to merit a Military Medal by the time of the Second World War. This is not to say that the former action did not deserve of recognition – just that we now have a hierarchy of medals available and can differentiate between degrees of bravery.

It is perhaps for this reason that no fewer than 111 Victoria Crosses were awarded in the short-lived and comparatively small-scale Crimean War (1854–1856) and 182 during the Indian Mutiny (1857–1859) whereas only 78 were gained during the Second Boer War (1899–1902), by which time other decorations were available. Not surprisingly, given the conditions and ferocity of the various campaigns, 628 VCs were awarded in the First World War (1914–1418) – the highest number in any campaign before or since. There were, of course, countless DSOs, MCs, DCMs and MMs and so on awarded as well.

What does this say about the Second World War, where just 182 VCs were awarded in 6 years of fighting – the same number as during the Indian Mutiny? Were there really fewer truly courageous acts performed in the Second World

War than in the First? Probably not: perhaps commanders were slower to recommend such an award or else the authorities were simply anxious not to diminish the value of the most prestigious decoration of them all. However, it is not the purpose of this book to delve into such tortuous matters, but merely to highlight those cases where Men of Kent and Kentish Men received their well-earned award.

It has been said that the Battle of Waterloo was won on the playing fields of Eton. Whilst this assertion (attributed to but denied by the Duke of Wellington) should be taken with a pinch of salt, it is remarkable how many of those who have been awarded the Victoria Cross over the years were educated at one or other of the major public schools. The list is impressive:

Eton	37
Harrow	19
Haileybury	17
Wellington	15
Cheltenham	14
Marlborough	13
Edinburgh Academy	9
Clifton College	8
Rugby	7
Dulwich	7
Stonyhurst	7
Westminster	7

(Source: *The Victoria Cross Society*)

Certain of these will be found in the pages that follow.

Some Victoria Crosses are retained by the recipient's family; many others are held in regimental museums and some by private collectors. The largest private collection is held by Michael Ashcroft's trust which, at the time of writing, holds 142 VCs. An indication of the intrinsic value of such a decoration may be gained by the fact that the first one bought by Michael Ashcroft, in 1986, cost him £29,000 (plus the buyer's premium and VAT). The prices today would be well into six figures.

In the pages that follow, the reader will find details of the circumstances that led to Victoria Crosses being awarded to men (so far no woman has ever been so decorated) who have a connection with the county of Kent. This may be through birth, family, residence, death and/or burial, although VC holders who just happened to be stationed in Kent at the time of their death have been disregarded unless there were other significant links to the county. Similarly, 'Kent' has been taken to include those parts of Metropolitan Kent that were included in the Administrative County before being swallowed up by the capital as a result of the London Government Acts of 1900 and 1963.

The book has been divided into six parts, covering the Crimean War, the Indian Mutiny, the late nineteenth-/early twentieth-century 'Colonial' wars, the Boer War, the First World War and the Second World War. The VC holders within these parts are listed chronologically, with as much detail of their lives, service and courageous deeds as it has been possible to ascertain.

They are all men of whom the county of Kent may be justly proud.

Chapter 1

The Crimean War

At first sight there may seem to be little connection between the frozen wastes of Russia and the scorching heat and dust of the Indian sub-continent but it must be remembered that Imperial Russia was an enormous country and had borders with Persia, Afghanistan and north-west India (now Pakistan) as well as Turkey and Europe.

In the middle of the nineteenth century, there were fears that Russia had plans to increase its sphere of influence and move in on the Ottoman Empire that spread from the Balkans, through Turkey and Palestine, to cover a large part of the Middle East. At the same time, there was a bitter dispute over certain religious differences between the Russian Orthodox Church and the Roman Catholic Church. These fears were heightened when, in the early 1850s, Tsar Nicholas I sent troops into Moldavia and Walachia (modern Romania), thus threatening the Balkans and Turkey, and by 1853 Russia and the Ottoman Empire were at war with each other.

The basis for the war, involving as it did various territorial and religious interests, was a complicated one and deeply concerned Great Britain and France. Britain feared a threat to India, to her domination of the Mediterranean and to the loss of Constantinople (now Istanbul) as a friendly port. At the same time, France was keen on making her own territorial gains as well as supporting the claims of the Catholic Church against the Russian Orthodox Church. Both countries therefore sided with the Ottoman Empire and, when a demand for the Tsar's troops to withdraw from Moldavia and Walachia was ignored, they both declared war on Russia.

It was the intention of the Allies to fight in two distinct theatres. On land, an Anglo–French army was sent to the Balkans, while the Allied fleet sailed for the Baltic. In both these theatres of war, British soldiers and sailors were to excel themselves despite sometimes confused and contentious leadership.

The Baltic theatre turned out to be something of a fiasco. With the Russian fleet refusing to leave port and do battle, the Allied fleet could only set up a blockade, the monotony relieved by a few desultory bombardments and a single, successful, all-out attack on the island of Bomarsund. It was during this blockade that Mate Charles Lucas won the first ever Victoria Cross.

Meanwhile, during the spring of 1854, the British Expeditionary Force (BEF) had set up bases in Constantinople and Scutari, only to witness the unaided Turks force the Russians to retreat, abandon Moldavia and Walachia and flee towards Bucharest. Not until September of that year did the British contingent, by now stricken with an epidemic of cholera, sail for the ominously named Calamita Bay some thirty miles north of their target, the Russian sea base at Sebastapol. The landing was unopposed and, with their French allies on their right, between the BEF and the sea, they began the march south towards their destination.

It was not to be an uneventful journey as they had to cross the River Alma, where the full might of the Russian army, under Prince Menshikov, awaited them with ninety-six cannons. The fact that Menshikov had been castrated by Turkish gunfire earlier in the conflict obviously did little to diminish his motivation or improve his humour. The ensuing battle was long and bloody but, after three days, the Allied forces had taken the Russian positions, winning six Victoria Crosses in the process.

The way was now open to Sebastapol, where the Allies contentiously set about establishing a formal siege, allowing the Russians time to block the harbour entrance and strengthen their defences. Not until 17 October did the Allied artillery commence the bombardment of the port.

While the Allies were thus fruitlessly employed, Menshikov saw an opportunity to attack Balaklava, the town near to Sebastapol from whence the British army was being supplied. A strong force of Russian infantry and cavalry began the assault around dawn on 25 October 1854 only to be repelled, largely by the 93rd Highlanders. It was during this battle that a misunderstanding of the Commander's orders led to the charge of the Light Brigade of cavalry. The story is too well known to merit repeating in detail here, suffice it to recall that during this engagement, which lasted less than half an hour, 110 men were killed, 130 wounded and 58 taken prisoner. What is remarkable is the fact that 375 men returned unscathed, 9 of whom were awarded the Victoria Cross, including Sergeant Major Charles Wooden, whose exploits are described later in this book.

The charge marked the end of the Battle of Balaklava. Even though the Russians had not taken the town, they regarded it as a victory, as they had successfully ruptured the British supply line at a time when winter was approaching.

With this battle out of the way, both sides concentrated their efforts on the siege of Sebastapol and, on 5 November 1854, the Russians launched a full-scale assault, on several fronts, in what was to become known as the Battle of Inkerman. Despite fierce fighting all around the town and port, the battle ended in stalemate: the Russians had failed to relieve the town and the Allies had failed to take it. It was to be nearly a year before the Russians finally decided to evacuate their positions in the town and thus ended the siege. It was also, to all intents and purposes, the end of the Crimean War, as a peace treaty was brokered by neutral Austria in March 1856.

It was in the January of that year, 1856, that Queen Victoria approved the design of the Victoria Cross, which was to be made from the bronze of two Russian cannons captured at Sebastapol. This unique gallantry medal was awarded to 111 veterans of the Crimean War, 6 of whom had connections with the county of Kent.

Mate Charles Davis LUCAS

Ulsterman Charles Lucas has the distinction of being the very first recipient of the newly created Victoria Cross, which he earned when he was just twenty. He was born on 19 February 1834 in County Armagh, Ireland, the youngest son of a wealthy land-owning Irish family with four sons and three daughters. The family home was in Clontibret, county Monaghan (where some accounts claim Charles was born). Lucas was proud of his Ulster origins and in later life demonstrated strong feelings against Home Rule for Ireland and supported the concept of Unionism.

In 1847, at the tender age of thirteen, he joined the Royal Navy as a cadet and distinguished himself in various naval actions during the Burmese campaigns of 1852–1853, during which he landed with storming parties and took part in the storming of the stockades and the capture of Rangoon, Dalla, Pegu, Prome and Meaday.

He had risen to the position of mate (senior midshipman) when, at the age of nineteen, he took part in Captain Lock RN's unsuccessful attack on the stronghold of the chieftain Mya Toom in which Captain Lock was killed and most of the senior officers killed or severely wounded. The force was obliged to withdraw and Mate Lucas took command of the rearguard, which was warmly engaged in keeping the enemy back during the nine-hour retreat. Mate Lucas was then almost continually employed in command of an armed boat up the River Irrawaddy in a most unhealthy climate.

In May 1854, having returned to England, he was appointed mate on HMS *Hecla*, a small steam-powered, paddle-wheel sloop or frigate which was to form part of the blockade that prevented the Russian fleet from leaving the Baltic port of Kronstadt during the Crimean War. The *Hecla* was to make a name for itself through its captain, Captain William Hutcheon Hall, deciding to ignore orders and bombard the island of Bomarsund on 21 June 1854. This was a particularly fruitless exercise since the shells made no impression on the strongly fortified bastion. The British commander, Sir Charles Napier, was furious at this waste of ammunition and complained that 'if every captain when detached chose to throw away all his shot against stone walls, the fleet would soon be inefficient'.

However, this inconsequential little action was rendered immortal by the actions of Mate Lucas. At the height of the action, while the *Hecla* and the island fortress were exchanging salvoes, a Russian shell landed on the deck of the *Hecla* with its fuse still burning. The crew were ordered to lie flat but Lucas showed 'a remarkable instance of coolness and presence of mind in action, he having taken up, and thrown overboard, a live shell thrown on board the *Hecla* while the fuse was burning' (Captain Hall to Admiral Napier, 22 June 1854).

As the shell hit the water it exploded, causing only minor damage and injury. Were it not for Lucas's prompt action, the consequences could have been disastrous. Lucas was immediately promoted to the rank of lieutenant and, when the Victoria Cross was instituted some two years later, Admiral Hall recommended Lucas. Lucas was gazetted with the award on 24 February 1857 and he attended the first investiture in Hyde Park on 26 June that year, when his medal was presented to him personally by Queen Victoria, together with a further 61 of the total of 111 recipients from the Crimean War.

The period of comparative peace in the immediate years following the Crimean War meant that Lucas saw no further action but he rose steadily through the ranks until he was promoted captain in 1867. He retired in October 1873 and two years later was promoted to rear admiral on the retired list.

Upon retirement, at the age of thirty-nine, the bachelor captain did not return to his native Ireland (the family lands and property presumably having been devolved upon his older brothers) but went to live with his sister and brother-in-law in the Western Highlands. However, this peaceful existence was interrupted in 1878 by a summons to the deathbed of his old captain, now Admiral Sir William Hall, who made a most remarkable request. In 1845, Hall had married the well-bred Honourable Hilare Byng, the third daughter of the Viscount Byng, who had been Hall's first captain, and whose family home was at Yotes Court, near Mereworth, Kent. With his dying breath, Hall beseeched Lucas to take care of his wife and, extraordinarily, to marry his only daughter, Frances. It seems Lucas was an incurable romantic for he agreed to his friend's dying wish and married Frances in 1879.

Although the union produced three daughters, it was not a particularly happy one. Frances was arrogant and had a violent temper; she was very conscious of her descent from the aristocratic Byng line, which included a number of admirals and generals, among them Admiral John Byng (1704–1757), executed (unjustly) for 'failing to do his utmost' to prevent Minorca from falling into French hands. The family would later boast Field Marshal the Viscount Byng of Vimy, who distinguished himself in the First World War.

The Lucas family settled in Tunbridge Wells in 1906, residing at Great Culverden in the Mount Ephraim area of the town. This great house, built by Jacob Fisher in 1830, no longer exists, having been demolished in 1927, and the site now forms part of the grounds of the Kent and Sussex Hospital. However, it remained the home of Rear Admiral Charles Lucas and his family at least until his death in August 1914 at the age of eighty. On his death, possibly at the instigation of his wife, his remains were interred at St Lawrence's churchyard, Mereworth, close to Frances's family home. The influence of the Byng family may be judged by the fact that Lucas's in-laws, Admiral Hall and his wife, are also buried there.

During his lifetime, Lucas was a staunch Unionist and also played an active role in the activities of the Tunbridge Wells Conservative and Unionist Association. He was a Justice of the Peace for both Kent and Argyllshire and it was during one of his many journeys to Scotland that he somehow managed to leave his medals in the railway carriage he had occupied. Despite an extensive search and appeals, they were never found, and probably lie in some private collection. Duplicates (including the Victoria Cross) were issued to him.

Surgeon James MOUAT

If Charles Lucas was the first VC of all, James Mouat has the distinction of being the first of thirty-six doctors to win this coveted award, going on to complete an illustrious medical career.

Of Scottish descent, Mouat was in fact born in 1815 – the year of the Battle of Waterloo – in Chatham, where his father, also an army doctor, was serving with the 25th Dragoons. He was educated at University College Hospital, London, becoming a Member of the Royal College of Surgeons in 1837 (Fellow in 1852). He followed his father's footsteps and joined the army, being appointed Assistant Surgeon to the 44th Foot (East Essex) Regiment in December 1838, with whom he saw service in India. In August 1839 he transferred to the 4th Foot (King's Own) Regiment and stayed in India – a move that probably saved his life as the 44th were posted to Afghanistan and were decimated during the notorious retreat from Kabul in 1842.

After nearly ten years in India, Mouat returned to England with his regiment, transferring once more, this time to the 9th (East Norfolk) Regiment of Foot, being appointed the regiment's surgeon in 1848. After the 9th Foot moved to Malta in 1854, Surgeon Mouat joined the 6th (Inniskilling) Dragoon Guards, with whom he went to the Crimea.

Surgeon Mouat served throughout the Siege of Sebastopol and was present in several engagements, including the battles of Inkerman and Balaklava. He was in fact was the Principal Medical Officer at Balaklava and it was there, on 26 October 1854, the day following the disastrous Charge of the Light Brigade, that Surgeon Mouat, in company with Sergeant Major Charles Wooden (see later), went to the assistance of Captain Morris of the 17th Lancers who was lying dangerously wounded in an exposed position after the retreat of the Light Brigade. Disregarding the severe enemy fire, the doctor reached Captain Morris and stopped a serious haemorrhage, thus saving his life. After dressing his wounds, still exposed to heavy rifle fire, James Mouat and Sergeant Major Wooden succeeded in bringing the casualty back to the British lines. For this action, Mouat was awarded the Victoria Cross.

The following year James Mouat was promoted to Surgeon Major and returned to England on half pay. In July 1857 he appeared before a commission, headed by Sydney Herbert who had been the Secretary at War at the time of the conflict, which had been formed to enquire into the appalling medical and sanitary conditions endured by the troops in the

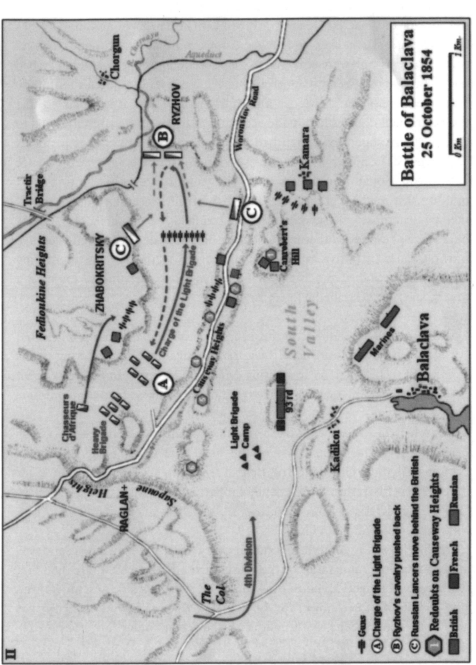

Map of the Battle of Balaclava.

Crimea and which had prompted a public outcry. He appears to have been given an easy ride by the commissioners, something he duly recognized by not rocking the boat. He said the only problem he had encountered was a lack of bricks to make an oven so that the troops could have hot food. However, three letters by him were attached to the subsequent report, in which he had complained about the sanitary problems. He was not questioned about these by the commissioners. There is no doubt that had Mouat complained that the regimental doctors had made recommendations and representations to their military superiors, which had been ignored, he would have seriously embarrassed the hierarchy – an unwise course of action for any career officer.

Surgeon Mouat nevertheless upset the famous Florence Nightingale by opining that medical officers serving at the front were more deserving of medals than those who served at the Scutari field hospital in Turkey. Nurse Nightingale responded that more doctors died at Scutari than had been lost in the Crimea (fifty-five members of the Army Medical Department died during the period of the 1854–1856 campaign). Never one to mince her words, she later described Mouat as:

> the typical clever fellow, the unscrupulous blackguard, the unmitigated rogue. I believe I need hardly say that, in all this, I am referring to his conduct to his men, as Inspecting Medical Officer. I do not refer at all to his medical practice; on which it is not my business to give an opinion.

In March 1858 Mouat went back on full pay and, two years later, to New Zealand, where he spent most of the next four years, being appointed Principal Medical Officer to the British troops in the New Zealand Wars. In 1864, on his return to England, he became the Inspector General of Hospitals and retired from the army in April 1876 at the age of sixty-one with the rank of Surgeon General.

In 1888 he was appointed an honorary surgeon to Queen Victoria and was made a Knight Commander of the Order of the Bath in 1894. He died of a stroke at his home in London on 4 January 1899 at the age of eighty-three. The *British Medical Journal* for 14 January 1899 carried an obituary that quoted the reminiscences of a colleague who served under Sir James:

> There was never a more thoroughly soldierly medical officer than Mouat; he was every inch military. A very dapper, well-made man, he was always

faultlessly dressed, whether in uniform or in mufti; nothing annoyed him more than slovenly or shabby attire, especially among medical officers. His rather brusque manner and strict military ways were on occasions somewhat unpleasant to those under him; but he was always their champion. If a little mild martinetism was permissible to himself, yet, if any outsider tried to bully a medical officer, he was at once up in arms. As an example of this, the writer can remember while Mouat was Principal Medical Officer at Aldershot and his office only thinly partitioned from the medical officers' library, overhearing him trouncing an officer of another department who had been discourteous to a young assistant-surgeon. He had a very sharp tongue, and as he usually got hold of the right end of an argument, was formidable in dispute. Himself an admirable regimental surgeon, he long favoured a return to the regimental system; but latterly, seeing that to be impossible, frankly accepted the corps autonomy with military titles. As he set no small value on himself or his military position, he always kept up considerable style, and was the only senior medical officer the writer can recall who made his camp inspections in a well-appointed carriage and pair.

Mouat's bold action that won him the Victoria Cross was not without certain questions and inconsistencies. Mouat claimed that he had to draw his sword to beat off some Cossacks but there is no evidence that any Cossacks reached that far up the valley and it was almost four years before his claim for an award was heard, by which time Lieutenant Colonel Morris had died in India. Sergeant Major Wooden's involvement went completely unrecognized until he wrote to Mouat, claiming that if he (Mouat) was to be decorated, then so should he. Mouat apparently agreed and forwarded Wooden's letter to Horse Guards, whereupon Wooden too was awarded the VC (see entry below). It has been suggested that Mouat's decoration was, at least in part, a reward for his silence during the post-war enquiry into the medical conditions in the Crimea.

James Mouat, the first doctor to be awarded the Victoria Cross, has been variously described as an ambitious, glory-seeking, sharp-tongued martinet but also as an energetic and skilful surgeon, devoted to the army and to the treatment and welfare of the troops under his control. A complex but undoubtedly courageous man.

Sergeant Major Charles WOODEN

Not a Kent man by birth, Charles Wooden was in fact a German national, born in London to German parents on 24 March 1827. At a young age he decided to join the British Army and enrolled in the 17th Lancers (Duke of Cambridge's Own). A large, ginger-bearded man, Wooden appears to have been quite a character and a source of amusement for his comrades, especially as he spoke with a strong German accent. One evening, after a heavy drinking session, Wooden returned to the barracks, only to be challenged by the guard who demanded the password.

'Tish me!' he cried.

The guard repeated his demand.

'Tish me, tish me, the devil!' responded the exasperated Wooden who had obviously forgotten the password. The sentry lowered his lance and pointed it at Wooden.

'Pass, tish me, the devil!' replied the sentry (who had probably known who he was all the time) and let him through.

Henceforward Wooden was usually referred to by his colleagues as 'Tish me the devil.' His regiment was based in England for many years but when the Crimean War began in 1854 it was promptly shipped out to that theatre of war, by which time the twenty-seven-year-old Wooden had risen to the rank of sergeant major.

During the Battle of Balaklava on 25 October 1854, the commander in chief, Lord Raglan, was angered to see the Russians removing British guns from an abandoned redoubt and sent an aide, Captain Nolan, to deliver an order to Lord Lucan, who was in charge of the cavalry:

> Lord Raglan wishes the cavalry to advance rapidly to the front, follow the enemy, and try to prevent the enemy carrying away the guns. Troop Horse Ailly [Artillery] may accompany. French cavalry is on left. Immediate.

The order was clear but, from where Lord Lucan was positioned, the redoubts were not visible and the only guns he could see were the twelve Russian guns of the Don Battery. An assault on these guns would be suicidal.

'Attack, sir? Attack what? What guns, sir?' exclaimed Lucan. Captain Nolan waved in the general direction of the Dom Battery and replied, 'There, my lord, is your enemy. There are your guns.'

Lucan passed the order on to his brother-in-law, Lord Cardigan, who commanded the Light Brigade. When Cardigan questioned the order, pointing out that the Russians had a battery of artillery immediately in front and batteries and infantrymen on either side, Lucan could only reply, 'I know it, but Lord Raglan will have it. We have no choice but to obey.'

And so, Cardigan led the 632 cavalrymen into what Tennyson was later to refer to as the 'Valley of Death', with Sergeant Major Wooden and the rest of the 17th Lancers – the 'Death and Glory Boys' – in the first line. Sergeant Major Wooden was perhaps lucky in that his horse was shot from under him in the early stage of the charge and he trudged his way back to the British lines on foot. Captain William Morris of the 17th Lancers reached the Russian lines where he was dismounted and badly wounded about the head before being taken prisoner. Despite his wounds, however, he managed to escape and rode off on a stolen horse before his new mount was shot from under him. Bleeding profusely from three deep head wounds, and with a broken arm and broken ribs, he staggered towards the British lines but eventually collapsed, coincidentally right beside the body of his friend, Captain Nolan, the officer who had brought the misinterpreted order to Lord Lucan, who had been killed at the very commencement of the charge.

Miraculously, a little over one half of the participants survived what seemed to be almost certain death and they were anxious to rescue those of their comrades who were lying killed or wounded in the valley, but the Russian artillery and rifle fire made any such attempt perilous in the extreme. Nevertheless, seeing his officer lying out there, obviously alive and in need of medical attention, Sergeant Major Wooden was quick to volunteer to go with Surgeon James Mouat of the 6th Dragoons to see if they could help him.

Ignoring the heavy fire aimed in their direction, they reached the unconscious Captain Morris, where the doctor dressed his wounds and splinted his arm, before he and Sergeant Major Wooden carried him back to the British lines. Because of the actions of these two men, Captain Morris survived, ultimately reaching the rank of lieutenant colonel before being killed four years later during the Indian Mutiny.

Around 1853, Charles Wooden married a Dublin girl, Eliza, and they had a son, Frank, born in Dublin in 1855, and a daughter, Lizzie, also born in Dublin four years later. Some accounts refer to there being two sons but only Frank is recorded in the 1871 census.

Wooden was promoted to Regimental Sergeant Major in April 1856 and served with the 17th Lancers in India during the Mutiny. As the years passed he probably had little thought of being decorated or otherwise rewarded for his action in the Crimea which, in the scheme of things, had not been a particularly hazardous one. He was therefore surprised to hear in 1858 – four years after the event – that Surgeon Mouat had been awarded the Victoria Cross for his part in their joint venture. No doubt feeling somewhat peeved at being ignored, he wrote to Mouat saying that if he (Mouat) was to get the VC, then so should he. Fortunately Mouat agreed and wrote to Horse Guards (the headquarters of the British Army in those days) recommending Wooden for the same award.

By this time four years had passed since the incident and the reply to Mouat's letter reads:

His Royal Highness feels very unwilling to bring any further claim for the Victoria Cross for an act performed at so distant a period but as the decoration has been conferred on Dr James Mouat for the part he took in the rescue of Lt. Col. Morris and Sergeant Major Wooden appears to have acted in a manner very honourable to him on the occasion and, by his gallantry, been equally instrumental in saving the life of this officer, His Royal Highness is induced to submit the case.

Wooden's VC was gazetted on 26 October 1858, the citation reading:

17th Lancers, Sergeant Major Charles Wooden

Date of act of bravery, 26 October 1854

For having, after the retreat of The Light Cavalry, at the Battle of Balaclava, been instrumental, together with Dr James Mouat CB, in saving the life of Lieutenant Colonel Morris CB of the 17th Lancers by proceeding under a heavy fire to his assistance, when he was lying very dangerously wounded in an exposed situation.

In October 1860 Wooden was promoted to the rank of Lieutenant and joined the 6th (Inniskilling) Dragoons as Quartermaster at the Mhow cavalry station in India. This was not a happy regiment and had a large turnover of field officers. It was also not a happy time for Wooden since, despite holding the VC, ex-rankers like him were not made welcome in the very class-conscious officers' mess. The following year matters worsened with the arrival of Colonel Henry Crawley as the commanding officer. Crawley quickly alienated most of his officers and was responsible for an incident that led to the death of the Regimental Sergeant Major. Over the next four years Lieutenant (QM) Wooden was called upon several times to give evidence before the enquiries and trials that followed. It would have been a great relief to him when he transferred to the 5th Lancers in 1865 and then into the 104th Regiment of Foot (Bengal Fusiliers) in 1871 when that regiment returned home from India.

Lieutenant Wooden's final years were spent with his regiment in Dover where he lived on the Heights with his wife and family, and it is here that he died under curious circumstances. For several days before his death he had been complaining of terrible headaches, although he continued to perform his duties as usual. On 25 April 1875 Mrs Wooden urgently summoned the regimental medical officer, Lieutenant Hooper, who promptly came to the Woodens' quarters where Charles Wooden's batman, Private Richard Kirby, told the doctor that his master had hurt himself. He said that he was bleeding profusely from the mouth and nose and, although Kirby had tried to get him to lie down, Wooden was too restless to do so. He kept pointing to his mouth and seemed to be trying to dislodge some object and said he had a tooth that needed extracting. It was clear that Wooden had been drinking heavily.

Lieutenant Hooper examined him and found that the roof of his mouth was severely damaged. He also noted that there were two cartridge cases on the floor of the room. The medical officer interviewed Mrs Wooden but she said she did not know what had happened, although she admitted she had picked up a small pocket pistol from the floor. It appears Lieutenant Wooden had bought this pistol in Dover a few days previously. Lieutenant Wooden remained alive and able to stand and talk for around twelve hours, after which, in the presence of the medical officer and Private Kirby, the patient succumbed to his injuries and passed away at four o'clock the next morning.

Just what had happened on that fateful day will never be known, although various hypotheses have been put forward. Was he so drunk that he tried to shoot out a painful tooth? Or was he suffering so much from either a bad tooth and/or his headaches that he had decided to end it all and take his own life? The coroner's inquest heard evidence that he had been suffering from depression and had suffered from sunstroke while serving in India and had been 'queer' ever since (although this may have been a further example of the attitude of his fellow officers to this outsider).

The verdict of the inquest jury was that Lieutenant Charles Wooden VC had taken his own life 'while in a state of temporary insanity' – a verdict which would not bar him from a Christian burial. And so Lieutenant Wooden's black coffin, bearing two bouquets of flowers and his hat and sword, was conveyed on a gun carriage to St James's cemetery. All his men attended the procession, as did most of the garrison's officers and three marching bands, as it made its way down Military Hill and along the Maison Dieu Road. The whole route was lined with townsfolk and many attended the actual burial. The service began in the cemetery mortuary but there were so many people attending that the men of his regiment had to wait outside with their caps removed.

As the coffin was lowered into the grave, to the accompaniment of three volleys of rifle fire, the chaplain referred to the deceased as 'a brave soldier who had upheld the honour and fame of England in many battles'. Wooden was just fifty years of age when he died. His medal is on display in the Queen's Royal Lancers' Museum at Belvoir Castle.

Lieutenant Mark WALKER

Mark Walker was born at Gore Point in County Westmeath on 24 November 1827. He was the eldest of three sons born to Captain Alexander Walker and his wife, Elizabeth. Captain Alexander Walker served with the 97th regiment (which later merged into the Queen's Own [Royal West Kent] Regiment) and distinguished himself in the Peninsular Wars in the early nineteenth century, in one instance saving the regimental colours by tearing them from the pole and wrapping them around his waist. One of his brothers (Mark Walker's uncle) was also an army officer.

Given this background, it is not surprising that Mark Walker chose a military life for himself, enlisting in the 30th (Cambridgeshire) Regiment of Foot on 25 September 1846. Unlike most newly appointed officers he did not have to purchase his commission because of his father's record.

When his regiment went abroad some five years after his appointment, Mark Walker remained behind as the adjutant at the depot in Walmer and, later, Dover – the first of his many associations with the county of Kent. He rejoined the regiment later and travelled with it to Cork and then to

Gibraltar. In May 1854, soon after Walker's promotion to lieutenant and adjutant, the regiment moved to Scutari in Turkey and eventually to the Crimea. The regiment fought in the Battle of the Alma, where Walker's horse was shot from under him and he was himself wounded, and then advanced to Sebastopol.

On 5 November 1854, the day broke miserably. It had been raining heavily and the ground was a quagmire. Worse still, as far as the troops were concerned, the area was shrouded in thick fog. Peering through the murk, the regimental pickets espied movement in front of them and gave the alarm. The 30th Regiment advanced in two battalions with Lieutenant Walker in the right-hand one under Colonel Mauleverer. The battalion had just come up to a low wall and lain down under its cover when, through the fog, two heavy columns of Russian troops appeared, almost on top of them. The order was given for the 30th to open fire but the result was no more than sporadic. In accordance with normal practice, the weapons had been piled overnight in front of the tents, but the stoppers for the rifles had become lost during the campaign and the weapons were wet and useless.

And still the Russians came on and the British troops, their ineffective weapons clutched in their hands, were becoming nervous to say the least. The situation was critical, but Lieutenant Walker seized the initiative. Ordering his men to fix bayonets, he leapt on to the low wall and, calling on the men to follow, charged towards the approaching Russians. The sudden appearance of the wildly screaming men, their bayonets gleaming in the morning light, unnerved the Russians, who had no idea how many others were lying behind the wall awaiting them. The Russians hesitated and then turned and fled, followed a short distance by Walker and his little band.

Walker's example and his cool and courageous conduct turned what might have proved a serious reverse into a brilliant episode of the battle and he was deservedly awarded the Victoria Cross.

Walker continued to lead his men throughout the harsh winter, spending the whole time in the trenches. In April 1855 he volunteered to lead a party that destroyed a Russian rifle pit that had been harrying the British troops. For this exploit he was mentioned in despatches, promoted to captain and transferred to The Buffs (Royal East Kent Regiment). On 9 June 1855, still in the trenches, he was severely wounded by shrapnel from a howitzer, which resulted in the amputation of his right arm.

With the cessation of the Crimean War, Captain Walker served with The Buffs in Ireland, India and China, where he was appointed brigade major.

He returned to England in April 1862 and remained in command of the depot at Canterbury when the regiment returned to India in 1857. Promoted to brevet lieutenant colonel in 1861 he took command of the 1st battalion of the Buffs in India before being appointed to command the 45th regiment (Sherwood Foresters) in 1873. In 1875 he was made a brigadier general and then major general in 1878, returning to England the following year.

All this time the fifty-one-year-old professional soldier had remained a bachelor but on 6 June 1881 he married Catharine Chichester in Arlington, Devon. Various military appointments followed and he reached the rank of full general in February 1893, at which point, just two months later, he retired from the army at the age of sixty-six. He was knighted (KCB) in the June of that year.

His affection for the county of Kent made itself manifest upon his retirement, he and his wife setting up home with two female servants and a manservant at 10 Castle Hill Avenue in Folkestone where he lived for the rest of his life. He was spending some time at his wife's family home at Arlington Rectory, Barnstaple, when, on 18 July 1902, at the age of seventy-five, he died. His body was returned to Folkestone where he was buried in the Cheriton Road cemetery. There is a memorial plaque in his honour in Canterbury Cathedral and his VC is held in The Buffs Museum in Canterbury.

Captain Matthew Charles DIXON

Matthew Charles Dixon was born to British parents in Avranches, Normandy, on 5 February 1821. His father was General Matthew Charles Dixon of the Royal Engineers (who somewhat confusingly bore the same names as those he conferred upon his infant son), while his paternal grandfather, Admiral Sir Manley Dixon, had a distinguished naval career prior to and during the Napoleonic Wars.

The young Matthew Dixon entered the army at the age of eighteen and trained at the Royal Military Academy, Woolwich, where young men were educated to take commissions in what were to become the Royal Engineers and Royal Artillery. Dixon was commissioned into the Royal Artillery, becoming a lieutenant in 1839 and rising to captain in 1848.

With the outbreak of war in 1854, Captain Dixon sailed to the Crimea with his battery, which was involved in the Siege of Sebastopol. It was during this operation that, around 2 pm on 17 April 1855, the battery commanded by Captain Dixon was subjected to a terrible cannonade and was virtually wiped out when an enemy shell struck the magazine. The resulting, devastating explosion destroyed the parapets, killed or wounded ten men, put five guns out of action and buried another with earth. Only one gun remained usable and, clearing the dust and debris off this, Captain Dixon helped and encouraged his few remaining gunners to reopen fire and himself acted as a member of the gun's crew. They continued firing until the light failed at dusk, around seven hours later, regardless of the concentrated fire from the line of Russian batteries and the ruinous state of his battery's position. For his actions on this day he was awarded the Victoria Cross.

A year later he was promoted to the rank of major and later to colonel. On 13 May 1862 he married Henrietta Letitia Eliza Bosanquet, the daughter of an admiral. They had no children.

In 1869, at the age of forty-eight, Dixon retired from the army with the rank of major general and he and his wife settled down in Pembury, near Tunbridge Wells, where they bought a substantial property known as Woodgate. The couple remained in this house and took part in local affairs until Major General Matthew Charles Dixon's death in 1905 at the age of eighty-four. He was laid to rest in the well-known Kensal Green cemetery, where so many famous people are buried. A memorial tablet to him can be seen in St Peter's Church, Pembury, where he and his wife were regular members of the congregation.

Major General Dixon's widow, some thirteen years his junior, survived him by twenty-one years and lived in the same Pembury house until her death in 1926 at the considerable age of ninety-two. Evidently the good Kentish air suited this gallant soldier and his lady.

Chapter 2

The Indian Mutiny

Ever since the beginning of British colonial rule in India, the native population had been concerned about the Westernization of the ancient, traditional Indian culture, be it Hindu, Muslim or other. The Hindu caste system was being eliminated and the British were keen to abolish the practice of *suttee* in which Hindu widows were expected to immolate themselves on their husband's funeral pyre. The other religions felt themselves equally threatened by the colonial rule.

These feelings were brought to a head when the Indian *sepoys* were issued with the new Enfield rifle. To load these it was necessary to bite off the end of the paper cartridges before pouring the black powder content into the barrel of the weapon. This would not have been a problem but for the fact that a rumour – correct or otherwise – that the cartridges were lubricated with lard to keep the content dry spread like a plague among these lowly troops. Lard is a product of either pigs or cows and to touch one's mouth with the product of either of these animals would have been a seriously sacrilegious act for any Hindu or Muslim.

The mutiny began in February 1857 when the 19th Bengal Infantry refused point blank to touch these cartridges. This revolt was quickly put down by the simple expedient of disbanding the regiment and replacing it with a British one. All was quiet then for a couple of months before the troopers at the Meerut garrison also rejected the cartridges. The eighty-five men concerned were sentenced to ten years' hard labour and dishonourable discharge from the army. The remaining Indian troops were incensed by this heavy-handed behaviour and lack of appreciation of their religious sensibilities and, waiting until the night following the imprisonment of their comrades, rose up and massacred most of the British in the garrison – officers, men, women and children alike. The mutineers were reinforced by other Indian troops and around 2,000 armed men marched on Delhi, leaving a trail of murder, rape, arson and looting in their wake. On 11 May the mutineers reached Delhi where they were joined by the *sepoys* from the town's garrison and a horrific orgy of death and destruction followed. Delhi was now firmly in the hands of the mutineers and news of the uprising soon spread to other parts of the country, inducing similar outbreaks across the whole of India. By 8 July 1857 the mutiny had spread as far south as Kolapore, where some 140 men of the 27th Bombay Native Infantry murdered three white officers and ran amok. Other officers and civilians were besieged in the residency while the mutineers took over a nearby stronghold.

The key to putting down the rebellion rested in the relief of Delhi and so a Delhi Field Force of 4,000 British, Sikh and Pathan troops, including the remnants of the Meerut garrison, set off for the town, where they were met by 30,000 mutineers. Despite the overwhelming numerical superiority of the rebels, the Field Force managed to secure a ridge to the north west of the city, where they continued to repel repeated attacks by the mutineers. But fatigue and sickness (cholera was rampant) meant the Field Force could not hold on indefinitely and so a relief column of mainly Sikh troops set forth to bolster the besieging force.

On arrival it was clear that, unless the city was taken very soon, the British and loyal troops would be too sick to attack and so it was decided that, even with a total of just 5,000 men, an assault would be launched to retake the city. Siege batteries were installed to provide breaches in the bastion's walls and eventually the main force attacked in five columns, aiming for the various shattered gates and breaches blown in the city walls.

There followed several days of confused and bloody fighting in which 1,254 British and loyal Indian troops lost their lives but, eventually, the attack succeeded and Delhi was recaptured, paving the way for the relief of Lucknow and the ultimate suppression of the mutiny.

Lieutenant William Alexander KERR

William Alexander Kerr was born in Melrose, Scotland on 18 July 1831 and by the time he was twenty-six was a Lieutenant in the 24th Bombay Infantry, stationed some seventy-five miles from Kolapore. He had already gained the reputation of being a fine horseman and had done much to promote racing in India and later published a number of works on riding and the supply of horses.

When the news of the Kolapore uprising was received, he volunteered to take fifty men from his regiment to relieve the situation, this being as many men as could be spared. Permission being granted, the little band needed barely half an hour before setting off to march to the scene. The monsoon was in full flow and the party had to cross five swollen rivers and a number of flooded defiles to get to their destination, but they did so in twenty-seven hours, albeit wet, muddied, hungry, thirsty and exhausted.

To take the rebel-held fort was going to be a problem given that Kerr had no artillery but, taking the bull by the horns, he decided on a full-frontal attack and selected just seventeen of his men to accompany him. As dusk fell they launched their assault on the stronghold, in which thirty-four fully armed mutineers awaited them. Setting fire to one side of the building, Kerr forced an entrance, while others broke down doors with the use of crowbars. Bullets were flying, one cutting the chain on Kerr's helmet, and another hit his sword. Temporarily blinded by a musket discharged near his face, Kerr recovered and ran his assailant through with his sword. While struggling to extract his sword, Kerr was struck on the head with a musket butt and was about to be bayoneted when a trusted subordinate came to his aid and shot the rebel dead. Recovering, Kerr struck down yet another mutineer.

Driven from the strongpoint, the mutineers made a stand in another building from which they were once more ejected, finally being overcome in a temple, which was burnt to the ground. Kerr and his men won the day, killing or capturing all the mutineers, but not without loss to themselves. Kerr lost eight men killed in the battle and another four died later from their wounds. Nevertheless, this action brought the mutiny on the Malabar coast to an end and Lieutenant Kerr was awarded the Victoria Cross for his 'dashing and devoted bravery'.

Not content to rest on his laurels, Lieutenant Kerr once again made a name for himself the next year when he was instrumental in preventing Tantia Topi, a rebel leader, from making a final attempt to resuscitate the failing rebellion. In 1860 he was a captain and the second in command of the Southern Mahratta Horse when he learned that the regiment was to be disbanded. Rather than seek a position with another regiment, Kerr decided to call it a day and resigned his commission. Sailing back to England, he married his wife Harriet the same year, and they eventually settled in Folkestone. The 1901 census shows them as lodging at 15 Clifton Crescent but they later lived at 82 Bouverie Road West until Kerr's demise on 19 May

1919 at the ripe old age of eighty-seven. It seems Harriet had predeceased him as there were only four mourners at his funeral in the Folkestone cemetery – his nephew and his wife and two officers of his acquaintance. Despite the meagre attendance, the *Folkestone Herald* reported that 'There were some beautiful floral tributes.'

His Victoria Cross is now held by the trust set up by Lord Ashcroft.

Bugler William SUTTON

William Sutton was born in Ightham in 1830 but his early life is somewhat shrouded in mystery. When the 1841 census was carried out, the eleven-year-old William was recorded as living with his brothers, James (aged twenty), Joseph (fifteen) and sister Dorcas (twelve) at an unnamed address in Borough Green. There is no mention of their parents and one can only assume that they had died and young James was the head of the family. Presumably the two elder brothers, who were listed as agricultural labourers, had to raise and maintain their two younger siblings.

It is not surprising, therefore, that as soon as he was old enough, William joined the army. It was a hard life but he had never been accustomed to luxury and at least he would see a bit of the world. By the time he was twenty-seven, he was serving as a bugler in the 1st Battalion, 60th Rifles (The King's Royal Rifle Corps) at Meerut, where the Indian Mutiny started. He and a few others were fortunate in being able to escape the marauding sepoys and the remnants of the 60th Rifles subsequently joined the Delhi Field Force. When the Field Force reached Delhi it was firmly in rebel hands and Bugler Sutton helped to man the ridge outside the city where the Field Force was entrenched.

Subjected to repeated attacks in force, Sutton distinguished himself by throwing himself wholeheartedly into the thick of the fighting. At one point, seeing an enemy bugler about to sound off a command, Sutton shot him dead, thus leaving the rebels vainly awaiting orders from their leaders. When the decision was made to invest the city, Sutton volunteered to go out and reconnoitre a breach that had been made in the walls to assess its suitability for an all-out assault. Throughout the campaign, Sutton showed 'conspicuous conduct' that even his peers recognized; when given the opportunity to elect one of their number for the Victoria Cross under Rule 13 of the Royal Warrant, his comrades chose Billy Sutton.

Not much is known of his life after the suppression of the mutiny. He seems to have left the army shortly afterwards and eventually returned to

England where he married a girl named Eliza. In 1871 they were living in Rotherhithe with their four children and the brave bugler was now a simple labourer. Ten years on William Sutton was living at his brother-in-law's house in Halling, near Rochester, with two of his children, aged five and eleven. He is shown as a widower and one assumes Eliza had died, possibly giving birth to the youngest son, Thomas, around 1876. William was now a bricklayer's labourer.

Sometime during the next seven years William Sutton returned home to Ightham where he died on 16 February 1888 at the age of fifty-eight. He lies buried in an unmarked grave in the churchyard of St Peter's Church, Ightham. A rather ignominious end for a brave man.

Private John FREEMAN

John Freeman was a true Kentish Man, being born in Barming/East Farleigh in 1833. Some records quote him as being born in Sittingbourne, but the census for 1841 shows him as living with his parents in Barming and as having been born there. John's father, Edward, was an agricultural labourer and by the time he was seventeen John had followed in his father's footsteps. By now the family were living at 50 Upper Stone Street, Maidstone which, although now situated well inside the borough, in 1851 would have been right on the outskirts and close to the great expanses of farming land around the town. The actual date of John's birth is unknown and, as is so often the case with the early, non-commissioned winners of the Victoria Cross, little is known about his life before, during or after his military service.

By the time he was twenty-four he had joined the 9th Queen's Royal Regiment of Lancers and was serving with that regiment when the Indian Mutiny broke out. The 9th Lancers served in several campaigns during the Mutiny, notably the siege of Delhi and the siege and relief of Lucknow. Their exploits won the respect of the mutineers who dubbed them 'The Delhi Spearmen', a name the Lancers were proud to carry.

In the autumn of 1857 the regiment was dispatched to Agra to help put down a revolt that had broken out there and, on 10 October, a fierce battle was fought between British troops and the mutineers. In the course of the fighting one of Freeman's officers, Lieutenant Jones, was wounded and in great danger of being butchered by the rebels. Without hesitation, Freeman rode to his assistance, killing the leader of the rebel cavalry, and defended the wounded officer against a number of the enemy. His courageous action was noted by his commander, Major General Sir John Hope Grant, who mentioned it in a despatch to London. Freeman's award of the Victoria Cross was gazetted in December the following year.

Private Freeman continued to serve in India following the Battle of Agra and was with his regiment on 5 May 1858 when the troops under the command of Sir C Campbell captured Bareilly. Private Freeman was dangerously wounded in the subsequent battle – the only British casualty!

Three years later, John had apparently been invalided out of the army and was back with his family, living at 1 Adelaide Place, King Street, Maidstone, and described as an invalid. Nevertheless, he evidently recovered from his injuries as he did not die until 1 July 1913 when he had reached the age of eighty. His movements in his later years are shrouded in mystery but it is known that he finally departed this life while living in Hackney, in the east end of London, and was buried in Stoke Newington cemetery.

Private Freeman's Victoria Cross is in the Michael Ashcroft collection.

Chapter 3

The Colonial Wars

The half-century or so between the end of the Indian Mutiny and the First World War was peppered with wars, battles, skirmishes and police actions in which soldiers and seamen fought bravely and fiercely for Queen and Empire. Apart from the Boer Wars, which are dealt with separately, Victoria Crosses were earned in places as far apart as Persia, New Zealand, China, Peshawar, Bhutan, Canada, the Gambia, the Andaman Isles, Abyssinia, Assam, Ghana, Malaya, Baluchistan, South Africa, Afghanistan, Zululand, Basutoland, the Sudan, Egypt, Burma, Manipur, the North-West Frontier, Matabeleland, Rhodesia and Tibet. Perhaps the reason the maps of the world at that time showed the British Empire in red was to represent the blood of the gallant British troops who fought and died in these far-off and now largely forgotten countries.

For the purposes of this book, we are only concerned with four of these campaigns: Zululand, the North-West Frontier, Sudan and Tibet.

The Zulu War (1879)
By the 1870s imperial fervour was at its height and, with parts of South Africa disputed by the Boers and the British, attempts were made to form a federal dominion of British Colonies and Boer Republics. To achieve this it was necessary for the British High Commissioner to control the Zulu lands bordering Natal and the Transvaal. Cetawayo, the Zulu king, refused to cede the land and so British troops under Lieutenant General Lord Chelmsford invaded Zululand in January 1879.

Thanks to the film *Zulu* and many books on the subject, the story of the massacre at Islandlwana and the subsequent stubborn defence of the Rorke's Drift mission station is too well known to need repeating here. Following the relief of Rorke's Drift, Chelmsford set off to relieve other troops who were besieged at Eshowe and suffering from disease and lack of supplies. On the way, on 28 March, the relief column ran into strong resistance at Hlobane Mountain but fought its way through and joined up with the beleaguered men.

With the two parties now joined, a concerted effort was made to overcome the Zulu resistance and, by the end of June, the British troops had reached the Zulu capital of Ulundi and the Zulus had capitulated. The war was over but at great cost and for little gain, since the planned British and Boer confederation was never achieved.

Major William Knox LEET

William Knox Leet was yet another of the many Irish-born soldiers who were to display great gallantry in the British army. Born in County Dublin on 3 November 1833, he joined the 1st Battalion of the 13th or Prince Albert's Regiment of Light Infantry (later the Somerset Light Infantry) and was a forty-five-year-old major at the time of the Zulu War. Major Leet has the distinction of being, as far as one is aware, the only holder of the Victoria Cross to have recommended himself for the award.

His regiment was part of Lord Chelmsford's column heading for Eshowe which, on 28 March 1879, ran into stout resistance around Hlobane Mountain (variously referred to as Inhlobana, Zlobane and Inslobane) and a group under the command of Lieutenant Colonel Redvers Buller, which had reached the high plateau, was forced to fight a rearguard action. This enabled a number of men to escape the Zulu hordes but, eventually, the group had to retreat down the mountain through a narrow defile known as the Devil's Pass, hotly pursued by the enemy. During the fierce fighting a number of men had their horses shot or speared from under them and were exposed to great danger. Colonel Buller personally saved two officers and a trooper and was accompanied by Major Leet and Lieutenant Edward Browne. The unhorsed soldiers included Lieutenant A Metcalfe-Smith, of the Frontier Light Horse, who had had his horse shot from beneath him, leaving him exposed to and pursued by a horde of Zulus. All seemed to be lost when Major Leet pulled the junior officer on to his own horse and raced back to the security of the British lines beneath a hail of bullets, assegais and other missiles. Both men were fortunately unscathed. Lieutenant Colonel Buller, Major Leet and Lieutenant Browne were all awarded the Victoria Cross for their bravery.

Lieutenant Metcalfe-Smith, understandably grateful to Major Leet for saving his life, made the following report to his superiors:

Kanbula Camp, 31 March 1879

I am most anxious to bring to notice that, in the retreat from the Inslobane mountain on the 28 inst., Major Leet 13th LI, who was quite a stranger to me, saved my life with the almost certainty of losing his own life by doing so. We were going along the top of the mountain, pursued by the Zulus, when Major Leet said to Col. Buller that the best way to get the men down was by the right side, and the Colonel said it was, and called out so to the men. However, everyone but Major Leet, myself and one other man, kept on to the front of the mountain while we began to descend on the right side. Major Leet and the other man were on horseback, but I was on foot, my horse having been shot. When we had got down a little way, a great many Zulus rushed after us and were catching us up very quickly – the side of the mountain was dreadfully steep and rugged and there was no pathway at all. They were firing and throwing their assegais at us while they rushed upon us. The third man was killed about halfway down.

While I was running by myself and trying to get away from the Zulus, who were rapidly catching me up, I turned round and shot one with my revolver. I was then quite exhausted and out of breath and intended to sit down and give up all chances of saving my life, as the Zulus were within a few yards of me. But Major Leet persisted in waiting for me, and called to me to catch hold of the packsaddle he was riding, which I did. Major Leet then finding that I could not keep beside the horse I was so done up and the hill so steep, insisted (though I told him it was no use) on stopping and dragging me up behind him on the horse, which was also greatly exhausted. By good luck, he escaped from the bullets and assegais of the Zulus and got near the Colonel's men, coming down from the rest of the mountain. Had it not been for Major Leet, nothing could have saved me, and I owe him the deepest gratitude, that I shall feel as long as I live.

A Metcalfe-Smith

This report was forwarded by Colonel Wood, whose covering report, as reported in the *Transvaal Argus* on 5 April 1879, included the following:

Major Leet, 44th Light Infantry, showed the most distinguished courage by helping on a dismounted officer, at the imminent risk of his own life. I should mention that Major Leet sprained his knee six weeks ago and can walk only with great difficulty.

(Signed) Evelyn Wood, Col.

Whether Major Leet was aware of his commanding officer's report or not, he was evidently not prepared just to wait and see what transpired. After all, the colonel's report did not appear to contain any recommendation for a decoration and could have resulted in merely a 'mentioned in despatches'. He therefore wasted no time writing to Colonel Goldsworthy, a contact and friend in a position to further his application for more tangible recognition:

Col. Wood's Column
Cambula Camp, Zululand

6 April 1879

My dear Colonel,

Before this reaches you the news of our big fights here will have reached you, and the despatches and newspaper accounts will have furnished you with the particulars. Thank God I have as yet escaped unhurt while so many good men have been killed. These Zulus are certainly terrible fellows – the finest specimens of humanity and the bravest men I have ever seen. Our work is still cut out for us and many a fine soldier will be lost before the war is over. I enclose copies of my reports. They will I feel sure interest you, and the General will probably like to look over them. I have I believe been fortunate enough to be mentioned in the official despatches. They all say here that I ought to get the VC for saving young Smith's life at the risk of my own, but Col. Wood being a VC man himself* (I do not know with what foundation) does not care to increase the number more than he can help. It is also said that there is an objection to recommending Field Officers but that seems absurd. I do not at all know myself whether I deserve it, but if I do it seems very hard that I should not get it. The

---

* Lieutenant (later Field Marshal Sir) Henry Evelyn Wood gained the Victoria Cross in India in 1859.

statement from young Smith was sent to Col. Wood. Do you think I deserve it? If so, can you assist me in the matter? You have connections with the Press, and in that way (of course without compromising me in any way) you might bring public opinion to bear. I think it likely that the '*Specials*' of '*The Times*' and '*Standard*' will report my case, and if so you could easily work it without compromising me. Remember I only ask you to do this if you think I thoroughly deserve it, otherwise I would not have it at any price. I feel quite sure I can entirely depend on you in this matter to act judiciously. I would of course give my eyes for a VC if outsiders think I deserve it and it would be a grievous blow to me if I deserve it and do not get it. I hope the General is quite well, remember me most kindly to him. Mrs Leet and Bertie are at … [?]. I have not seen them since August. Rowlands and Harvey are lamentable failures on active service. I wish you were out here with command. You are too good a friend to think this matter I put in your hands too much trouble – with my kind regards, believe me

I am very sincerely yours,
W Knox-Leet.

Major Leet's efforts bore fruit and he was awarded the Victoria Cross for his actions. In July 1881 he was promoted to lieutenant colonel and was in command of the second battalion of the Prince Albert's Somersetshire Light Infantry when the Third Anglo–Burmese War broke out in 1885. The battalion was involved in some fierce fighting and lost 144 men in this short-lived conflict. William Knox Leet went on to become a major general before retiring in 1887.

Sometime around 1870, Major William Knox Leet married Charlotte Elizabeth Anne Sherlock, the daughter of an important Irish family from County Cork. They had two sons: Bertie, who was born in Ireland in 1874, and Dudley, who was born in Devon in 1881. Sometime between the birth of Dudley and the 1891 census Charlotte died and Major General Leet was recorded as living in Isleworth, Middlesex with just a housekeeper and maid for company. He later moved to Great Chart, near Ashford, Kent where he died on 29 June 1898 at the age of sixty-five. He is buried in St Mary the Virgin churchyard, Great Chart, where there is a memorial to him.

The North-West Frontier

This region, between Afghanistan and what is now Pakistan, has been a problem area for centuries, certainly all the time the British had an interest in the area. The actual frontier between the two countries was the subject of considerable dispute and a British commission finally drew up the line of demarcation. This brought many frontier tribesmen under British colonial influence, much to their dissatisfaction, which they expressed most violently by rising up against the British frontier garrisons.

In August 1897 Mohmand tribesmen attacked Shabkadar but there were enough troops in the area to deal with this and two divisions under Brigadier General Sir Bindon Blood proceeded to the scene of the uprising. On 14 September the column was attacked while camped for the night but fought off the attackers and advanced the next day to join battle with the rebels in the Mohmand Valley. Three more columns under Brigadier General Jeffreys moved up to join their comrades in the valley, making a substantial military force that nevertheless met with strong opposition. Although suffering considerable casualties, the British force proved too strong for the rebels, and the uprising in that particular region was crushed.

Corporal James SMITH

James Smith first saw the light of day in 1870 or 1871 in the Kent county town of Maidstone. As the child of a working-class family, little is known of his early days, and with a name as common as Smith it is very hard to trace any records outside his military exploits.

What we do know is that, when he was probably just old enough, he enlisted in the Royal East Kent Regiment (The Buffs) and rose through the ranks to gain his second stripe by the time he was around twenty-six.

Having spent a little time in Singapore, the 1st battalion of The Buffs sailed for India to start their fourth tour of that country in January 1887. Their red tunics with the buff facings had been abandoned some time since, in favour of the more practical khaki drill. The first few years of their posting were spent training and playing sport but it was not too long before they were called upon to do some real soldiering on the North-West Frontier. While stationed at Peshawar in the searing hot month of July 1897, the regiment was ordered to form, with three Indian battalions, Brigadier General Jeffreys' 2nd Brigade that was to support Sir Bindon Blood's force, which was under attack by a large force of Pathans in the Malakand. The arrival of this relief brigade enabled the rebels to be overcome and Blood sent Jeffreys off to deal with the fierce Mahmund tribe to the north west.

Having arrived at the scene, on 16 September 1897, the brigade embarked on a punitive sweep up the Mahmund Valley, causing the tribesmen to take to the hills where they enveloped a regiment of Sikhs. Companies of the Buffs hurried to their assistance and then continued their advance before withdrawing back to their camp.

By now they had been on the go since early morning with nothing more than a hard-tack biscuit to eat – a situation that sorted the men from the boys. Winston Churchill, who was riding with the column as a correspondent, reported: 'The older and more hardy amongst them laughed at their troubles. The younger ones collapsed in all directions. The officers carried their rifles. Such ponies and mules as were available were laden with exhausted soldiers.' (In fact, it was probably more the after-effects of fever that caused the men to collapse rather than their youth.)

By the time the Buffs reached their encampment, it was dark, but Lance Corporal James Smith and ten men from G Company were not among them: they had volunteered to go back and look for a wounded officer. Instead they came across their commander, Brigadier General Jeffreys himself, who, with a handful of Indian sappers and two Royal Engineers subalterns, was pinned down outside the walls of the burning village of Bilot. The little group of Buffs was welcomed into the makeshift leaguer with open arms, for it was being subjected to a hail of stones, burning bales of straw and bullets. Under these circumstances it was impossible to withdraw, taking with them the four artillery pieces and the wounded men, and the occupants of the leaguer had to shelter behind whatever cover they could find: dead mules, boxes, panniers, rocks and so on. Lance Corporal Smith was amongst those who received wounds but he coolly carried on firing his rifle, encouraging his comrades and helping to move the wounded back to what little shelter there was. With the two officers and such men as were able, Smith took part in a bayonet charge in an endeavour to clear the village of the enemy.

By the early hours of the morning, two of the Buffs were dead, five were too badly wounded to be able to take any active part and only four were still able to fire, albeit exhaustedly. One can only imagine their relief when a full company of Sikhs arrived and drove off the enemy.

The two Royal Engineer officers were awarded the Victoria Cross but, as is so often the case, the junior NCO was overlooked and it was not until seventeen months after the incident that his courage was equally recognized, and even then only after the matter had been raised in Parliament. Four of the Buffs privates were decorated with the Distinguished Conduct Medal.

James Smith continued to serve in The Buffs, eventually retiring with the rank of colour sergeant. He returned to his home county and died in Dartford on 18 March, 1946, aged seventy-five, having lived through the Boer War and two World Wars since his days on the North-West Frontier.

The Sudan Campaign (1896–1900)

The assault by dervishes on the besieged town and garrison of Khartoum in 1895, resulting in the wholesale massacre of the defenders and most of the 34,000 civil population, including General Gordon, was viewed as a major disaster back home in Britain and there was a clamour for revenge. But not until a new Tory government under Lord Salisbury had been elected was any action taken. By this time there were growing concerns about the Khalifa's rule in the Sudan, which bordered British-controlled Egypt, and so General Sir Herbert Kitchener, who was the Sirdar (commander in chief) of the Egyptian Army, was dispatched to retake control of the Dongola Province in Sudan. Kitchener accordingly led a combined force of Egyptian, Sudanese and British troops into Sudan and occupied Dongola in September 1896. The laying of a railway line the following year caused the Khalifa to threaten action so Kitchener sent for more troops and soon had an army of 26,000 at his disposal. This great force continued their advance towards the Khalifa's base at Omdurman (nowadays a suburb of Khartoum) and, by September 1898, was within artillery range of the town. Kitchener deployed his force in an arc close to the bank of the Nile, where gunboats already were waiting to play their part. There was a wide, flat plain in front of him with hills on either side and he placed his cavalry on either flank.

For some reason the Khalifa made the grave tactical error of bringing his 46,000 men out of the town. Eight thousand infantrymen with rifles and spears, under Osman Azrak, came out on to the plain facing Kitchener's forces, while the remainder were deployed out of sight in the hills. Around 6am on 2 September Osman Azrak launched his attack, closely followed by a further 8,000 dervishes, similarly armed. A quarter of these were completely wiped out by artillery fire before they even came within range of the rifles and Maxim guns and the remainder fared little better. Attempts at flanking moves received similar short shrift.

With his forces severely mauled, the Khalifa started to withdraw back towards Omdurman and Kitchener brought his men out from their defensive positions and proceeded to march towards the town. It was established practice that, before advancing into country hidden from view behind a hill, the cavalry should be sent on ahead to look over the top and report any hazards, and so Kitchener sent the 21st Lancers on ahead to reconnoitre.

They soon saw a group of several hundred dervish horsemen facing them, apparently with the intention of stopping their further progress. Colonel Martin ordered the 300 or so lancers to proceed and they fell foul of a favourite Arab ploy – a deep depression behind the dervish horsemen concealed around 2,000 fresh dervish troops. The dervish horsemen opened fire on the cavalrymen and, confident that they could sweep away the enemy horsemen, the four squadrons of 440 lancers lined up some 300 yards from their opponents, forming a line covering almost a quarter of a mile. Colonel Martin gave the order and the 21st Lancers spurred their horses to make what was, unknown to them, probably the last major cavalry charge in history.

All did not go well with them. As they topped the rise at full gallop they suddenly came upon the massed ranks of dervish infantrymen in the depression. Even had they wanted to, there was no way they could have stopped, and they were soon amongst the white-robed enemy, lashing out with lance and sword against rifles, spears and broad-bladed swords.

Once through the dervish lines, with twenty-one of their number dead and around sixty-five seriously injured, the Lancers regrouped, galloped around the enemy flank, dismounted and engaged them with their .303 Lee-Metford carbines. Their deadly accurate fire deterred the mass of dervishes and they withdrew. Among those taking part in the charge was the young Winston Churchill who was attached to the 21st Lancers and later wrote of the brave deeds he had witnessed.

The Khalifa threw more men into the battle from various points and fighting continued for the rest of the morning but, faced with superior artillery and massive firepower that killed 11,000 of his troops and wounded 16,000 more, the battle was ultimately lost. The opposition collapsed, allowing Kitchener to march triumphantly into Omdurman, and Gordon's death had been avenged at long last.

Private Thomas BYRNE

Thomas Byrne was born in Dublin on 9 December 1867 and, like so many of his countrymen, escaped from the poverty that blighted Ireland by joining the British Army. The Irish are noted for their love of horses and equestrian skills so it is perhaps not surprising that he chose the cavalry and enlisted in the 8th Hussars in 1886, transferring to the 21st Hussars a year later. The regiment served unremarkably in India from 1887 and moved on to Egypt in 1896, changing its name the following year to the 21st Lancers. There was little time for the regiment to train in the use of its new weapons, the nine-foot-long lances, before it was ordered to the Sudan as part of Kitchener's Anglo-Egyptian force, charged with preventing the French from occupying the country or, as the newspapers preferred to describe it, 'Avenging the death of General Gordon.'

A smart man with a luxuriant, waxed moustache, Byrne does not appear to have been an outstanding soldier, being still a private after around a decade of service, but his bravery can never have been in question. During the Battler of Omdurman, described above, when the 21st Lancers were called upon to charge the enemy, he did not hesitate and, although wounded, was amongst the horsemen fighting desperately with the thousands of heavily armed dervishes concealed in the depression or *khor*.

A bullet wound to the right arm that caused him to drop his lance did not deter 'Paddy' Byrne and, although the last man to enter the *khor*, he did so at its widest and most heavily defended sector. The Lancers' horses were slaughtered by the horde of dervishes as they stumbled into the depression, being stabbed by spears and slashed with swords, while the unhorsed troopers were similarly hacked to death by the fanatical and merciless tribesmen.

Hearing a cry for help, Byrne turned and saw Lieutenant Molyneux of the Royal Horse Guards (who had voluntarily joined the charge after conveying Kitchener's orders to the Lancers) surrounded by dervishes. Molyneux also was wounded in the arm and, unhorsed, unarmed and streaming with blood, he was in imminent danger of a terrible death. Wheeling his horse around, Byrne charged the enemy, giving the officer a chance to make good his escape. Because of Byrne's wound his right arm was disabled and his sword, dangling uselessly from his hand, was knocked from his grasp, rendering him effectively unarmed, and he received yet another wound, a spear being thrust into his chest. A sword slash across his back was fortunately deflected by his bandolier and he carried on, perhaps a little desperately, for this was literally a case of 'do or die', and eventually managed to escape from the bloody mêlée.

Weak and dizzy from loss of blood, Private Byrne was led away three miles to where there was a dressing station where his wounds could be treated. He was later conveyed by hospital barge to Cairo, as was Lieutenant Molyneux. While in hospital Molyneux was visited by his friend, Lieutenant Winston Churchill of the 4th Hussars, who had been attached to the 21st Lancers for the campaign. Molyneux was in need of a skin graft and, when a nurse declined to provide one, Churchill stepped in and later wrote: 'I managed to hold out until he [the doctor] had cut a beautiful piece of skin with a thin layer of fresh attached to it. This precious fragment was then grafted on to my friend's wound.'

As for Private Byrne, he too recovered from his wounds, although he never fully regained the full use of the fingers of his right hand. His bravery was brought to the attention of his superiors and also to the public at large when Winston Churchill (who was also acting as war correspondent for the *Morning Post*) wrote of Byrne on 16 September 1898, 'The bravest man I have ever known.' Private Thomas Byrne was awarded the Victoria Cross for his courage, as were two of his officers, Captain Pail Kenna and Lieutenant de Montmorency (the son of General the Viscount de Montmorency). Presentation of the awards to the three was made by Queen Victoria at Osborne House whence the two officers were conveyed by royal carriage. They later dined with the Queen, whereas Paddy Byrne travelled by hackney carriage and shared his dinner below stairs with the servants.

The Sudan campaign was over by the end of 1899 and the 21st Lancers returned to Britain for service in Ireland, but Montmorency sailed for South Africa to take part in the fight against the Boers and Paddy Byrne went with him as his servant. Although they intended to join the Imperial Light Horse, they were compelled by circumstances to join another unit before Montmorency managed to raise a force known as 'Montmorency's Scouts', comprising local men who were fluent in Bantu and Afrikaans as well as being excellent horsemen and keen shots. This unit of some eighty-five men saw service in various battles and skirmishes but during the course of one such conflict in 1900 Montmorency was shot dead. Byrne was desolate and had to be restrained from riding out to recover the body.

Byrne returned to Dublin to rejoin his regiment and it was here that he met and married Bridget Pender, by whom he was to have eight children.

When the regiment moved to Canterbury the newlyweds set up their home there and it became their adoptive home for the rest of their lives.

On 19 September 1910 Private Byrne retired from the army. The couple occupied various homes in Canterbury, including one in East Street, and by 1914 Byrne was living at 30 Notley Street where he remained for nearly thirty years, until his death.

On 16 November 1914 Byrne joined The Buffs as an 'Army Reserve (Special Reservist) ... for one year only, unless the war lasts longer in that case, until the end of the war.' He described himself as a pensioner on the attestation form and declared that he was forty-eight and married. His writing and spelling was extremely poor, suggesting his education had been very limited (that might account for his lack of advancement in rank). He repeatedly signed his name as 'Bryen' – an error which was corrected by the attesting officer – and referred to his wife as 'Bridjet', the way it is spelt on her grave.

After the war, Byrne worked as a messenger at the Canterbury Cavalry Depot until he retired in 1931, having been in the service of the Crown for forty-six years. He devoted his retirement to gardening and the work of the British Legion and often marched at the head of the annual Remembrance Day parades, usually in company with fellow VC holder William Traynor (referred to later).

Bridget predeceased him by five years, dying in February 1939 at the age of sixty, after which Byrne moved in with his daughter Norah in St Gregory's Road, Canterbury. In 1942 he was knocked down by an army despatch rider, breaking a leg. He never really recovered from this last setback and died on 15 March 1944 at the age of seventy-seven. He was afforded a full military funeral, his coffin being conveyed on a gun carriage through the crowded Canterbury streets. Both he and 'Bridjet' are buried together in a recently restored grave in the Westgate cemetery, Canterbury.

Thomas 'Paddy' Byrne left his Victoria Cross to his eldest son, Edward, who apparently lost it while serving in Uganda during WW2. It has been suggested that the VC that Idi Amin used to sport with other medals during his dictatorship was Byrne's, but this has never been confirmed. When Edward died, his son petitioned Queen Elizabeth II for a replacement to be issued, which was granted. Just two years later this replacement was auctioned off, prompting the Queen to declare that she would never again sanction the issue of a replacement VC.

The Tibet Campaign, 1904

Often described as the 'Jewel in the Crown' of the British Empire, India was also a source of considerable problems and anxiety. One major cause of concern was the growth of Imperial Russia's influence in the Far East. Throughout the nineteenth century, Russia had made steady advances eastwards, threatening India itself. Although Britain had a degree of influence in the border countries of Sikkim, Bhutan and Tibet, it did not occupy them and rumours that Russian representatives had visited Lhasa, the capital of Tibet, caused alarm bells to ring in Whitehall. To counter any possible Russian influence in the area, the British government sent a frontier commission to negotiate with the Tibetans, which met with delay and obfuscation. Eventually the Viceroy of India, Lord Curzon, authorized a diplomatic mission, accompanied by an escort of 1,150 men, to go to Lhasa and 'coax' the Dalai Lama to come to the negotiating table.

This mission set out in December 1903 but was not a happy one because of the clash of personalities between the leader of the mission, Lieutenant Colonel Frances Younghusband, an experienced Himalayan explorer, politician and intelligence officer, and the commander of the escort, Colonel JRL Macdonald of the Royal Engineers. Macdonald had a reputation as an arrogant, petty and overly cautious officer and, although his role was purely a military one, he constantly interfered and sought to undermine the authority of Younghusband, his military junior.

After more than three months' march the mission reached the village of Guru where a large but essentially ineffective Tibetan army blocked their advance. Initially this resistance was countered peacefully, but the shooting of a Sikh soldier by the leader of the Tibetans prompted the British to open fire with overwhelmingly greater firepower which, coupled with the Tibetans' reluctance to leave the scene, resulted in nearly half the Tibetan force of 1,500 being killed and many more injured.

Fighting their way through yet another obstruction, the British mission came to the undefended Gyantse citadel, built on top of a 500-foot rocky outcrop, with the town scattered around its base. The British mission set up camp in some old buildings, known as Chang Lo, about a thousand yards from Gyantse, from where Younghusband sent messages calling upon the Tibetans to allow them to continue to Lhasa. Typically, his efforts remained unanswered, and Macdonald decided to withdraw more than half the escort to the base camp because of the lack of supplies.

Exasperated, Younghusband sent the energetic Colonel Brander, with some 350 of the remaining escort troops, to disperse a concentration of Tibetan soldiers around 50 miles away, leaving just 120 riflemen to protect the main mission at Chang Lo. Taking advantage of the situation, a party of some 800 Tibetans attacked Chang Lo but, after a fierce battle, were repulsed by the mainly Sikh and Ghurkha escort. Smarting from this setback, the Tibetans moved some 6,000 troops into the Gyantse citadel from where they conducted a desultory siege of the mission in Chang Lo. An order was sent to Macdonald to bring the main escorting troops up from the base camp to Chang Lo in preparation for an assault on the citadel.

On 6 July 1904 the British troops marched into Gyantse and cleared the mean shanties that comprised the town in preparation for the assault on the citadel high above them. After an artillery barrage, the Royal Fusiliers and the 8th Gurkhas commenced their climb and successfully routed the Tibetans. This incident, in which Captain Grant won his VC, was the turning point and the mission was able to proceed to Lhasa where a treaty was signed and the British withdrew.

Lieutenant John Duncan GRANT (Tibet 1910)

John Duncan Grant was born in India on 28 December 1877, where his father, Colonel Suene Grant, was serving with the Royal Engineers. He was sent to England to be educated, first in Hastings and subsequently at Cheltenham College. At the age of eighteen he entered the Royal Military College, Sandhurst, being commissioned in January 1898. His first appointment was with the 30th (Punjab) Regiment of the Bengal Infantry, being promoted to lieutenant in April 1900 and transferred to the 44th (Gurkha Rifle) Regiment, later renamed the 8th Gurkha Rifles.

In 1903 the young lieutenant's regiment provided part of the escort to the Younghusband mission to Tibet. After assisting in the various skirmishes which involved the mission, they arrived at Chang Lo, from where they were selected to take part in the assault on the sheer flanks of the Gyantse outcrop to clear the citadel of the Tibetan occupants.

On 6 July 1904 the British artillery commenced a bombardment of the fort, eventually creating a breach in the thick curtain wall, followed by the explosion of the fort's magazine. This provided the awaited signal and, accompanied by Royal Fusiliers, the 8th Gurkhas began to scale the rocky cliffs. The Gurkhas – more accustomed to the altitude and more adept at this type of work – soon pulled ahead, despite a barrage of rocks and fusillades from the Tibetans' ancient matchlocks.

Maintaining his position at the head of his troops, Lieutenant Grant and Havildar (Sergeant) Karbir Pun eventually reached a position just beneath the breach that the artillery had created in the wall of the citadel. In single file and on hands and knees they managed to reach the breach before the lieutenant was hit and they were driven back. Calling for covering fire, the intrepid pair attacked the breach once more and, followed by the remainder of the troops, entered the fort and routed the occupants. The fort was now in British hands and, with the Tibetan resistance overcome, the mission was able to proceed with its diplomatic overtures.

The bravery of Lieutenant Grant and his companion was recognized by the award of the Indian Order of Merit to Havildar Karbir Pun (the VC was not open to members of the Indian Army until 1911) and the Victoria Cross to Grant. His citation in the *London Gazette* read:

> On the occasion of the storming of the Gyantse Jong on July 6 1904, the storming party, headed by Lieutenant Grant, on emerging from the cover of the village, had to advance up a bare, almost precipitous rock face, with little or no cover available, and under heavy fire … One man could only go up at a time, crawling on hands and knees to the breach in the curtain. Lieutenant Grant … attempted to scale it but, on reaching the top, he was wounded and hurled back, as was also the Havildar, who fell down the rock some thirty feet. Regardless of their injuries, they again attempted to scale the breach and, covered by the fire of the men below, were successful in their object, the Havildar shooting one of the enemy on reaching the top. The successful issue of the assault was very greatly due to the splendid example shown by Lieutenant Grant and Havildar Karbir Pun.

Returning to England for an extended leave, Grant married Kathleen Mary Freyer in London before returning to India and being promoted captain. The couple had a son, Hugh, and a daughter, Madeline.

By the time the First World War broke out, Grant was a brigade major and was again wounded in Mesopotamia (Iraq). After service in France and Belgium in 1917, he returned to Egypt and Mesopotamia once more, where he was promoted to acting lieutenant colonel to take charge of the

3rd battalion of the newly formed 11th Gurkha Rifles. This new regiment (which was disbanded in 1922) was then posted to India and saw action on the North-West Frontier where Lieutenant Colonel Grant was awarded the Distinguished Service Order.

Promoted to full colonel in 1926, Grant's last appointment was as Deputy Director, Auxiliary and Territorial Force, India and he retired in 1929 with a Companion of the Bath to add to his impressive array of ten medals and decorations. In 1934 he was appointed Honorary Colonel of the 10th Gurkha Rifles and during the Second World War he served in the London District Home Guard Command.

After a stay in Brighton the Grants moved to Tunbridge Wells where they lived for a number of years, the Colonel dying in the Fraserley Nursing Home, Park Road, Tunbridge Wells on 20 February 1967 at the age of 89 – the oldest living VC holder at the time. On 7 July 2009 a small ceremony saw a tree being planted and a memorial plaque unveiled to Colonel Grant in the Kent and Sussex Crematorium, Tunbridge Wells, where his ashes had been scattered.

Chapter 4

The Boer Wars (1880–1902)

The title of this chapter is given in the plural since there were in fact two Boer Wars: the first was a fairly short-lived one, lasting merely a matter of months. Despite a humiliating defeat for the British Army, it saw a number of courageous actions by its members.

At the end of the 1879 Zulu War tension between the British imperialists and the Boers (Dutch/Afrikaans for 'farmers') was mounting because of the failure of the British government to return the Transvaal, which it had annexed, to the Boers. This, coupled with objections to the taxation imposed and alleged indiscipline of the British troops, led to the Boers declaring a republic on 16 December 1880.

Four days later a party of 257 men of the 94th Regiment of Foot (Royal Welsh Volunteers) was ambushed and suffered 57 men dead and more than 100 wounded, all the survivors being taken prisoner. (The 94th was later amalgamated with the 88th to form the Connaught Rangers.)

The seven British garrisons in the Transvaal were quickly surrounded and the Boers prevented the 2,000 troops in Natal from marching into the Transvaal to relieve them by blocking the route across the Drakensberg at Laing's Neck. Attempts to dislodge the Boers were repulsed, with severe casualties being inflicted on the British. Further battles ensued with the British being generally outsmarted by the Boers and the High Commissioner for South-East Africa, Major General Sir George Pomeroy, was killed.

Reinforcements under Brigadier Sir Evelyn Wood arrived in March 1880 with orders to seek an armistice and the Pretoria Convention was signed that same month, giving the Boers independence under British sovereignty.

The Second Boer War was a more prolonged event. By the end of the nineteenth century the British had subjugated the natives in South Africa and had set up the colonies of Natal and Cape Colony. The Boers had control of the two republics of Transvaal and Orange Free State but the discovery of gold in the Transvaal had resulted in the two republics being overwhelmed by foreign settlers (mainly British) whom they referred to as 'Uitlanders'.

Moves by the British to combine the British colonies and the Boer republics into a British-dominated South African Federation were strongly opposed by the Boers. When negotiations broke down, the Boers seized the initiative and invaded Cape Colony and Natal in October 1899, besieging the British garrisons of Ladysmith, Mafeking and Kimberley, thus beginning a war that would last nearly three years and cost Britain dearly in both monetary and human terms.

This pre-emptive strike by the Boers was the first of three distinct phases. The second phase began when the British troops, under Field Marshal Roberts, called up more troops and began a series of counteroffensives. Having secured Natal and the Cape Colony, the British invaded the Transvaal, capturing its capital, Pretoria.

The third and final phase began in March 1900 when the Boers began a protracted and fierce guerrilla campaign, which prompted the British, now commanded by Lord Kitchener, to respond by embarking on a scorched earth policy, destroying Boer farms and placing civilians in concentration camps. This provoked outrage back home and the public, already tired of this seemingly pointless war, were calling for an end to hostilities. This finally came in 1902 with the signing of the Treaty of Vereeniging which, although bringing the two Boer republics into the British Empire, forced the British to make a number of concessions and pay substantial reparations to the Boers.

Private John DOOGAN

It was during the first and short-lived Boer War that Private John Doogan won his Victorian Cross. An Irishman, like so many other soldiers in the British army, he was born in County Galway in March 1853 and joined the army as soon as he could, enlisting in the 1st King's Dragoon Guards. By 1879 the regiment was in South Africa where, following the withdrawal of the 17th Lancers, it was the sole imperial cavalry unit and much in demand for scouting, escorts and communications. The following year most of the regiment set sail for India but a troop of the King's Dragoon Guards, under Major Brownlow, was held back pending their return to England. Private John Doogan was at this time acting at Major Brownlow's servant.

However, the disturbances in the Transvaal led to the troop's embarkation being suspended and Major Brownlow was instructed to gather together a cavalry squadron for immediate active service in South Africa. Not without great difficulty, he managed to scrape together a squadron consisting of around a hundred mounted men, drawn from the 60th Rifles (later the King's Royal Rifle Corps), the 58th (Rutlandshire) Regiment of Foot and the Army Service Corps, plus some twenty-five Dragoons. Brownlow had considerable difficulty in finding mounts for these men as it was the practice for troops leaving one foreign posting for another, or to go home, to sell off the vast majority of horses before they left, and this is what had happened to those belonging to the Dragoons. The infantry were naturally inexperienced horsemen and, as one disdainful cavalry officer wrote, 'T [Tommy] Atkins cannot shoot well on foot, and on horseback it takes all he knows to keep his seat.' Nevertheless, this ad hoc force was an essential part of the attack at Laing's Nek, their job being to charge to the left of the Boer lines and take a small hill, still known as Brownlow's Kop, to protect the flank of the 58th Regiment.

The charge took place on 28 January 1881 with all the élan expected of a cavalry assault with Major Brownlow in the lead, accompanied by the troop of Dragoons, with Sergeant Major Lunny and Corporal Stevens close by. As they reached the ridge the two NCOs were both killed (the only fatal casualties in the battle) and the major's horse was shot dead, he himself being wounded. Nevertheless, the gallant officer continued to fight and shot the leader of the Boers with his revolver. He continued to urge his men on but the leading troop was now exhausted and their three leaders were either unhorsed or dead. The following mounted infantry, through a combination of lack of horsemanship and the use of mounts untrained for the noise of shooting, were unable to provide the necessary support, resulting in the impetus being lost and the whole assault falling away. This one failed incident led to the ultimate defeat of the British at Laing's Nek as it exposed the infantry in the valley to fire from both the front and the flank and they had to withdraw.

During the attack, Private Doogan, seeing his officer unhorsed and in great danger, leapt from his own horse and insisted that the major take it, being twice wounded in the process. It was this brave act that earned him the Victoria Cross.

Little is known of the subsequent movements of Private John Doogan, VC. At some point he evidently left the army, married and set up home in England and enjoyed a long life. When he died in 1940 at the age of eighty-six, he was living at 5 Folly Road, Folkestone, and was buried in the Shorncliffe Military Cemetery.

Second Lieutenant John NORWOOD

John Norwood was born on 9 September 1876 and named after his father, who was a merchant living at Pembury Lodge, Beckenham, although the family were originally yeomen from Stilstead in the parish of East Peckham, Kent. John junior went to school in Beckenham and was then educated at Rugby and Oxford.

On 8 February 1899 John Norwood joined the 5th (Princess Charlotte of Wales's) Dragoon Guards and was almost immediately dispatched with his regiment to South Africa where the Second Boer War began in October of that year. The regiment at that time was commanded by Lieutenant Colonel Robert Baden-Powell, who was to become famous as the founder of the Boy Scout movement.

A large force of British troops had been assembled in the colony during the preceding months, most of which was deployed around the garrison town of Ladysmith, but this show of force failed to impress the Boers, who sent an even larger force of 21,000 into Natal from several directions. An attempt to capture the Boer artillery by the whole of the British force at Ladysmith was an abysmal failure with the loss of 1,200 British troops, the remainder, including the 5th Dragoons, being forced back into the town, which the Boers promptly besieged. Although a prompt relief was anticipated, the siege actually lasted 118 days.

There were periodic skirmishes and probes by both sides during the siege and, on 30 October 1899, a small patrol of the 5th Dragoon Guards, commanded by Second Lieutenant Norwood, went out from Ladysmith and promptly came under heavy fire from a large force of the enemy who were entrenched on a ridge. The cavalry patrol got to within 600 yards of the ridge before the withering gunfire caused them to retire at full speed. During this withdrawal one man dropped and Norwood turned and galloped back some 300 yards, still under heavy fire. On reaching the unhorsed trooper, Norwood dismounted and, picking up the fallen man, carried him out of range on his back, at the same time leading his horse with the other hand. It was for this act of bravery that he was awarded the Victoria Cross.

Following the relief of Ladysmith and the eventual ending of the Second Boer War, John Norwood continued with his army career, reaching the rank of captain before joining the Reserve of Officers in February 1911 at the age of thirty-five. He married and settled down to a quiet existence which lasted for just three years since with the outbreak of the First World War he immediately rejoined the regiment and went with it to France as part of the BEF – the 'Old Contemptibles'. His renewed service was to be short, however, since he lost his life during the First Battle of the Marne on 8 September 1914 – less than a month after the outbreak of war. He was laid to rest in the Communal Cemetery in Sablonnières, France.

A brass memorial plaque dedicated to Captain John Norwood, VC, and to his relative, Second Lieutenant John Norton Norwood, who died on the Somme, has been erected in St Michaels Church, East Peckham, referring to the fact that they were 'kinsman who constituted the sixth generation made of the yeoman family of Norwood, sometime of Stilstead [farm] in this Parish'.

An untimely end for a young hero with strong ties to the county of Kent.

Lieutenant Henry Edward Manning DOUGLAS

Henry Douglas first saw the light of day on 11 July 1875 in the somewhat unprepossessing environs of the Brompton Convict Prison in St Mary's Vale, Gillingham, where his father, George Douglas, was a warder. The family (there were at least six children) lived in the Warders' Quarters at the prison. Six years later George Douglas was appointed Chief Warder at Woking Prison and the family moved to 20 Prison Street in that town, where young Henry continued his education.

Despite his humble background and no doubt cash-strapped family, Henry somehow managed to qualify as a doctor, and in July 1899 entered the newly created Royal Army Medical Corps. He had little time to assimilate any military training as by December of that year he was with the army in South Africa where war had just been declared by the Boers.

Lieutenant Henry Douglas wasted no time in getting 'blooded' as, on 11 December 1899, he was present during the military action at Magersfontein where the Boers had laid a trap and, concealed in well-hidden trenches, awaited the arrival of the fatigued British troops. The result was a disaster for Britain, whose troops were soundly beaten and had to retire to lick their wounds.

During the engagement, Lieutenant Douglas showed great gallantry and devotion to duty, going out into the open under very heavy fire to attend to Captain Gordon of the Gordon Highlanders, who was badly wounded. Ignoring the bullets whizzing around him, the young doctor coolly went about his mission of mercy, attending also to the wounds of Major Robinson and a number of other men lying wounded in the open, completely disregarding his own safety. Throughout the day he continued to provide treatment to and care for the exposed wounded men. For his courage in this action Lieutenant Douglas was awarded the Victoria Cross, to which the Distinguished Service Order was later added.

Henry Douglas was promoted to captain in 1903 and continued to serve in Africa with only a short break in England. He rose to the rank of major in 1911 and, while serving in the First World War, was promoted to lieutenant colonel. His postings took him to Iraq and Karachi and from 1926 to 1929 he was the commandant of the Royal Army Medical College. He left the army in 1933 with the rank of major general – a considerable achievement in those days for the son of a humble prison officer from Ireland. Major General Henry Edward Manning Douglas, VC, CB, CMG, DSO, QSA, Croix de Guerre, died in Droitwich on 14 February 1939. He was sixty-four years of age.

Captain Walter Norris CONGREVE

The name of Congreve is a distinguished one in military circles and Walter Norris Congreve maintained the traditions of a family that included two distinguished eighteenth-century artillerymen: Lieutenant General Sir William Congreve and his kinsman, also Sir William Congreve, who developed the Congreve rocket, used widely during the Napoleonic Wars.

Walter Norris Congreve was born in Chatham on 20 November 1862, the son of Captain William Congreve, JP DL, who was a regular officer in the 9th (East Norfolk) and 29th (Worcestershire) Regiments of Foot and later became the chief constable of Staffordshire (1866–1888). Walter was educated at Harrow School and Oxford University but failed to graduate, having left after a senior member of the college was wounded with an air rifle. This perhaps was the first sign of Congreve's passion for shooting and musketry that served him so well in his later career.

Already an officer in the North Staffordshire militia, he joined the regular army in 1883 and, on completion of his training at Sandhurst Royal Military

College in 1885, he was commissioned as a second lieutenant in the Rifle Brigade and served with the 4th Battalion in India. The regiment returned to England in 1889 and the following year he married Cecilia Henriette Dolores Blount La Touche, the daughter of an officer in the Indian army.

By the time the Second Boer War began Congreve was a captain and was serving on the staff of General Sir Redvers Buller VC. On 15 December 1899, during an assault at Colenso, the artillery brigade under Colonel Charles Long unprecedentedly pushed ahead of the infantry and came under heavy fire. Several of the gun crews either became casualties or were forced to retire, leaving their guns behind in the open and well within the range of the Boer marksmen. In a situation closely similar to that which applied at the time of the Charge of the Light Brigade, nearly half a century earlier, General Buller called for volunteers from his staff to ride out and try to rescue the abandoned guns. Captain Congreve was one of the first to offer his services and was joined by two aides-de-camp, Captain Harry Norton Schofield and Lieutenant the Hon 'Freddy' Roberts (son of Field Marshal Lord Roberts, VC). They were also accompanied by Corporal George Edward Nurse of the Royal Field Artillery.

Mounted on a troop horse, his own having vanished in the confusion, Congreve and his two brother officers together with a handful of other ranks galloped across half a mile of open countryside with two gun limbers, raked with shell and rifle fire, and had almost reached the guns when Congreve was wounded in the right leg and elbow. His clothing was pierced by several other bullets and his horse was killed so he took shelter in a hollow, or *donga*, with the remnants of the artillery brigade, where they remained under a blazing sun for several hours without food or water. Schofield and Roberts and the other ranks managed to limber up two of the guns and recover them but Lieutenant Roberts was hit in the stomach and lay mortally wounded on the sun-scorched veldt. With the aid of Major William Babtie of the RAMC, Congreve hobbled over to where Roberts lay and together they managed to carry him to the relative safety of the *donga*.

In the late afternoon the Boers chivalrously called a truce so that the dead and injured could be recovered and Congreve and Roberts were among the wounded brought back to the British lines, where Roberts died two days later. Congreve, Schofield, Roberts, Babtie and Nurse and two others were all awarded the Victorian Cross for their actions in this battle (posthumously in the case of Lieutenant Roberts).

Having recovered from his wound, Captain Congreve continued to serve in South Africa and later in Ireland and Malta, advancing through the ranks to full colonel. In September 1909 Colonel Congreve was appointed the commandant of the School of Musketry in Hythe where he greatly improved rifle skills, raising the rate of fire to fifteen aimed shots a minute. In September 1914, now a brigadier general, Congreve took his command to France where his training methods were put to the test – so rapid was the rifle fire of the British infantry that the German troops opposing them believed they were facing machine guns.

Advancing to the rank of major general, Congreve was the only corps commander to be wounded during the war, having his left hand shattered by shrapnel while on a visit to Vimy Ridge in June 1917. The hand was later amputated. While recovering at home, Major General Congreve was knighted and promoted to lieutenant general in charge of XIII Corps.

As a corps commander, Congreve was not an unqualified success. He was never a well man, suffering from asthma and bronchial troubles, and the loss of his son, Major William La Touche Congreve, VC, on the Somme affected him deeply. Although his senior officer, General Sir Hubert Gough, found that 'there were few generals in the British Army who surpassed him as a commander' others regarded him as being 'not dashing enough' and Haig was known to question his efficiency. Before the Battle of the Somme two of Congreve's divisions were removed and attached to the XV Corps but his remaining two divisions were the only ones to take all their objectives in the July 1916 offensive, earning him Haig's grudging congratulations. In fact, Congreve's personal courage cannot be doubted, but, as he wrote to his son in 1916, 'I don't feel I can ever make a general for I cannot face having men killed in the ruthless way generals must do,' and this avowed disinclination to endanger his troops may have led to the slurs of reluctance to fight.

Congreve's next appointment as GOC VII Corps was possibly a promotion too far and his tactics during the German offensive in March 1918 proved disastrous. In April 1918 General Gough was removed from his command of the 5th Army and the following month his subordinate, Lieutenant General Congreve, was ordered home, Haig refusing to see him.

After the Armistice, Congreve served in the Middle East where he expressed a dislike for Socialists, Irish nationalists, Arabs, Jews and Syrian Christians in equal measure, writing in a letter to Sir Henry Wilson 'they are all alike, a beastly people, the whole lot of them not worth one Englishman'.

Nevertheless, his latest command was judged a success and the dry, warm climate suited him.

Retiring as a full general, he was appointed governor of Malta in June 1924 and died there on 28 February 1927, being buried at sea. The baronetcy that was due to be conferred on him at the time of his death at the age of sixty-four was instead conferred on the elder of his two remaining sons. There have been only three cases of father and son both being awarded the Victoria Cross: Walter Congreve and his son, William (killed on the Somme in 1916); 'Freddy' Roberts and his father Lord Roberts; and Sir Charles Gough (Siege of Delhi) and his son John Gough (First World War).

Lieutenant Francis Newton PARSONS

Francis Parsons was a true Man of Kent, being born in Dover on 23 March 1875, the son of Dr Charles Parsons, a surgeon who lived at 2 St James Street in that town. He was one of at least eight male and four female children, no fewer than three of whom (Raymond, Guy and Godfrey) were lieutenant commanders in the Royal Navy. Another brother, Courtney, was a doctor who died of fever in South Africa.

Francis was educated at Dover College and King's College, Cambridge before entering Sandhurst. He joined the Essex Regiment in February 1896, serving in the 1st Battalion, and was promoted to full lieutenant in March 1898.

In February 1900 he was serving with the regiment in South Africa as the tide of war was beginning to turn in favour of the British. Kimberley was relieved and Ladysmith soon followed while, in the west, the Battle of Paardeberg resulted in eventual surrender of the Boers. It was during this, one of the last battles of the war, that Lieutenant Francis Parsons distinguished himself. One of his men, Private Ferguson, was wounded and, while trying to crawl to safety, was again hit in the stomach and was left lying in an exposed position in full view and range of the Boer marksmen. Undaunted, Lieutenant Parsons went out to him and dressed his wounds as best he could and reassured him. He returned twice to bring the injured man badly needed water from a nearby river before finally hoisting his comrade up and carrying him to safety, all the while the two men were under heavy fire from the enemy.

Parsons' courage was rewarded by the recommendation for the Victoria Cross but, although the award was approved and made, he never lived to receive it. On 11 March 1900, some three weeks after the Paardeberg incident, twenty-five-year-old Francis Newton Parsons died at Dreifontein from wounds he received in that later battle in which he displayed 'conspicuous gallantry'. He was buried in Dreifontein cemetery where his brother officers erected a headstone to his memory. There is also a commemorative tablet in St Mary's Church, Dover, where the family used to worship. The family presented his medals to the Essex Regiment museum at Warley, Essex, in 1962.

Corporal Frank Howard KIRBY

Frank Kirby was born in Thame, Oxfordshire on 12 November 1871, the son of a self-employed and apparently comfortably-off ironmonger, receiving his education at Alleyn's School, Dulwich, an important fee-paying secondary school. On leaving the school he was employed by his father as a travelling salesman, while his younger brother was also employed by their father as a tinsmith and brazier.

However, it would seem that the life of an ironmonger's salesman was not to Frank's liking for in 1892, at the age of twenty-one, he joined the Royal Engineers as a private soldier or sapper. When the Second Boer War broke out in 1899, Corporal Frank Kirby went with his regiment to South Africa where, in March 1900, he was awarded the prestigious Distinguished Conduct Medal for his part in blowing up the Bloemfontein Railway. Not content with this, in June of the same year Corporal Kirby was with a party that had been sent to try to cut the Delagoa Bay Railway. When they were near Bronkhorstspruit, Pretoria, however, they were forced to retire, being hotly pressed by a very superior number of the enemy. While the rearguard was in the process of pulling back, one of the men, whose horse had been shot, was seen running after his comrades. He was a long way behind the rest of the rearguard troop and was under brisk fire. Observing the man's plight, Corporal Kirby turned and rode back to the man's assistance. By the time Kirby had reached the exhausted soldier the enemy was pressing closely and both men were subjected to heavy fire at close range. Ignoring the shot and shell whizzing around them, Corporal Kirby managed to get the dismounted man up behind him on his horse and ride over the next rise which was held by the rearguard and where they were out of view and range of the enemy.

As well as receiving the DCM, Corporal Kirby had already been mentioned in despatches for his courageous acts and lack of concern for his own safety, and his nomination for the Victoria Cross was approved. He also received a field promotion to troop sergeant major (from corporal) in July 1900. He received the Victoria Cross from the hand of the Duke of Cornwall in August of that year.

By the end of 1901 he was back in England and served tours of duty as a company sergeant major and quartermaster sergeant instructor before being made a warrant officer in 1906 and appointed the regimental sergeant major at Brompton Barracks, Chatham. In 1909 he married Kate Jolly and they produced two sons and two daughters, but this did not distract Sergeant Major Kirby from his military career. In April 1911 he was commissioned from the ranks and Lieutenant (QM) FH Kirby was posted to the newly formed Air Battalion of the Royal Engineers at Farnborough, moving on to the Royal Flying Corps the following year as squadron commander. He became the stores officer at the Central Flying School at Upavon and went to France in 1916. On 1 January 1917 he was promoted to captain in command of the Army Aircraft Park at Trevent. He then commanded No 1 Stores Depot at Kidbrooke with the rank of major and became the Inspector of Stores Depots as a lieutenant colonel. Ultimately, when the Royal Flying Corps (RFC) was assimilated into the Royal Air Force in 1918, he took command of the Technical Group of that new service as a full colonel. His rank became that of group captain when the rank structure was changed. He received an OBE in 1919, which was upgraded to a CBE in 1926. On retiring from the Royal Air Force, Frank Kirby became the managing director of a construction waterproofing company.

Group Captain Frank Howard Kirby, VC CBE DCM died in Sidcup on 8 July 1956 at the age of eighty-four, having risen from the rank of sapper to that of group captain – a remarkable feat for the one-time ironmonger's salesman. There is a memorial to him in St Barbara's Garrison Church, Chatham.

Private William J HOUSE

Born in Thatcham, Berkshire on 7 October 1879, William House was the only son of an agricultural labourer and his wife, Thomas and Sarah House. Thomas House had served in the army and was now a reservist and so, given this background, it was not surprising that William wasted little time in joining the military to escape the prospect of grinding rural poverty. Given his place of birth, it was equally unsurprising that he opted for his county regiment, The Royal Berkshires (Princess Charlotte of Wales's Own), and duly enlisted on 3 November 1896 at the age of seventeen.

With the outbreak of the Second Boer War, the regiment was soon in South Africa and was heavily involved in the fighting around Mosilikatse Nek on 2 August 1900. During the fighting, companies A and B of the Royal Berkshires were ordered to climb a steep position under heavy resistance from the entrenched Boers. On reaching the top, a Sergeant Gibbs was sent forward to reconnoitre, but he was soon spotted by the enemy, who opened fire and severely wounded him.

Despite advice not to do so, Private House went out under heavy fire to help the sergeant, who was lying in a very exposed location. The advice proved to have been sound for, as he reached the wounded man, Private House was himself quickly hit by soft-nosed bullets and seriously wounded in the neck and/or head. Now fully aware of the dangers, he called out to his comrades not to attempt to rescue him but to leave him where he and his comrade lay, in full view of the enemy and within range of the Boer riflemen, while he did what little he could for the seriously wounded NCO. When the main body advanced towards the Boer positions shortly afterwards, both Private House and the sergeant were rescued and removed to receive medical attention. Unfortunately, despite Private House's administrations, Sergeant Gibbs did not survive. Private House's selfless actions had not gone unnoticed and he was recommended for the Victoria Cross, which was awarded on 7 October 1902.

House's head injuries seemed to have been satisfactorily treated and he continued to serve with his regiment until 1904 when his seven-year term of service expired and he was placed on the reserve list. Civilian life obviously did not appeal to House and soon rejoined his old regiment which, because of his VC, welcomed him back with open arms. He served in the Sudan and then in India where he was promoted to lance corporal and transferred to the 1st Battalion, which was garrisoned in Dover's Grand Shaft Barracks. By this time, Lance Corporal House was showing signs of mental problems, and a colleague, Lance Corporal Stroud, who had known him before he went to India, later stated that when House came back from India he was a changed man. 'There was a terrible change in him. From being lively and talkative he had barely a word to say to anyone and would mope about round his cot a great deal.' Whether his problems arose from his head wounds or some form of post traumatic stress resulting from his service either in South

Africa or in India will never be known. Certainly he suffered severe fits of depression, although this did not prevent him from carrying out his duties such as drilling new recruits, a task he did not particularly enjoy.

On 28 February 1912, unnoticed by the other soldiers in the same barrack room who were engrossed in watching a parade, House quietly attached one end of his pull-through to a bed post and the other end to the trigger of his rifle. Standing up, he placed the muzzle to his head and tugged the weapon. A bang, and it was all over, and his startled comrades turned from the window to see Lance Corporal House dead on his cot with half his head blown away.

An inquest was held in Dover before which Lance Corporal Stroud and others gave evidence as to House's state of mind before his death and it was also disclosed that, although the unmarried House had been corresponding with an unknown young lady, no letter from her could be found after his death. Did this relationship have any bearing on House's decision to do away with himself? We shall never know.

The coroner returned a verdict of suicide during temporary insanity and Lance Corporal William House VC was buried in St James's cemetery, Dover with full military honours, including a firing party. Curiously, the grave was not marked until 1994, when his regiment had a headstone erected over the spot where he lay.

Sergeant William Bernard TRAYNOR

William Bernard Traynor started life on the last day of 1870, in Hull, East Yorkshire, the son of Francis Traynor, a hemp dresser living 29 Moxon Street, and his wife, Rebecca. Certain sources claim that Francis Traynor was born in Ireland and claim his son's VC as being awarded to an Irishman. There is no doubt, however, that William was born in Hull and the 1881 census shows his father, Francis, as also being born there. The same census does list other men also named Francis Traynor and of similar age, who are shown as being born in Ireland, and it is perhaps here that some confusion has arisen.

Like many others, in similar towns and lacking money, education or prospects towards the end of the nineteenth century, William enlisted in his county regiment, the 2nd Battalion of the West Yorkshire Regiment (Prince of Wales's Own), in November 1888, and spent much of his early military career in India. It appears William Traynor returned to England for at least a short time, since he got married in Maidstone in 1897.

In 1899, with the commencement of the Boer War, he found himself with his regiment in South Africa and, on 6 February 1901, was heavily engaged in an attack on Bothwell Camp. During the battle, Sergeant Traynor (as he now was) saw a comrade lying wounded in the open and so, leaping out of his trench, he ran to his aid. Traynor did not have a charmed life, however, and by the time he reached the wounded man he had a shell splinter in his chest and a bullet in his thigh. Thus largely incapacitated he was unable to carry the other wounded soldier unaided but Lance Corporal Lintott came to his assistance and, between them, they managed to carry their colleague back to the British lines. Despite his undoubtedly painful injuries, 'Traynor remained in command of his section, cheering his men and encouraging all by his devoted example, until, finally, the attack failed and the enemy drew off.' The *London Gazette* carried the notice of the award of the Victoria Cross to Sergeant Traynor on 17 September 1901, while Lance Corporal Lintott received a Distinguished Conduct Medal.

Such were the conditions in South Africa at the time that Sergeant Traynor's bride, Jane, was notified that he had been killed in action. This proved to be somewhat premature since, although his wounds were sufficiently severe to merit his being invalided out of the army, he was to enjoy life for another fifty-three years! Repatriated to England, Sergeant Traynor's wounds made it impossible for him to go to Buckingham Palace to receive his Victorian Cross from the King in person, and it was not until 1920 that he was able to travel to York to receive his medal from Colonel Edward Stevenson-Browne, himself the holder of a Victoria Cross.

On being invalided out of the army in 1902, the Traynors settled in Dover and William began a long and active relationship with the town. He obtained a post as orderly room clerk with the Royal Artillery at Dover castle, moving on to become a barrack warden until he finally retired in 1935. Although obviously unfit for active service during the Great War, he still earned a mention in despatches for his 'valuable services in connection with the war'.

William Traynor's involvement with the life of the town included playing an active role in the local branch of the British Legion and he was a notable freemason. For many years he had the honour of laying the British Legion's poppy wreath at the town's war memorial each Remembrance Day. In 1951, the fiftieth anniversary of the award of his Victoria Cross, the town of Dover honoured him with a civic dinner in the town hall with music provided by the band of The Buffs. Two years later he was one of the few non-Freemen invited to a Coronation lunch held also in the town hall by the Hereditary and Honorary Freemen of the town. It is very evident that, besides being a very brave man, William Traynor was a much-respected and well-loved citizen of his adopted town.

By now, William Traynor's long life was coming to its end. His wife had died twenty years before and, on 20 October 1954, William Bernard Traynor, VC died in Buckland Hospital, Dover at the age of eighty-three. The funeral at St Andrew's Church was attended by a large congregation, including the mayor and other local dignitaries. As the coffin was lowered into his grave, beside his wife and young son, a bugler sounded the Last Post and Reveille while the black-draped military standards were lowered in respect for 'one of England's great gentlemen'.

Although they lost one son at the age of twelve, Jane and William Traynor had a total of six children in all, their twin boys following their father into the army and both finishing up as majors in the Royal Engineers.

Given the esteem with which he was regarded during his lifetime, it is sad to note that in 2003 William Traynor's grave and headstone were found to be in a disgraceful state and a band of local volunteers set about rectifying the matter, commenting: 'It's a great pity that in the first place, the people of Dover allowed his grave to deteriorate like this ...' His medals are held privately.

Chapter Five

The First World War (1914–1918)

The origins of the First World War (or the 'Great War' as it was known at the time and up until the commencement of the Second World War) are, as is the case with most conflicts, very complex. The assassination of Archduke Ferdinand in Sarajevo on 28 June 1914 was simply the flash point for various grievances, imperial ambitions and other festering problems throughout Europe. So far as Britain was concerned, it was the violation by Germany of Belgium's neutrality that brought her into the escalating conflict. The invasion was part of Germany's so-called Schlieffen Plan, which was designed to overrun France via Belgium before the British came into the war. With France neutralized and the British army locked in the British Isles, Germany would be able to turn her attention to Russia. But determined resistance by the Belgians slowed the German advance and very soon hopes of keeping Britain out of the war were dashed. On 3 August 1914 Great Britain declared war on Germany and, the next day, on Austria-Hungary. By 20 August the BEF, a formidable body of highly trained, experienced (South Africa and other colonial conflicts) regular soldiers was in action at Mons where they faced an enemy more than twice their size. However, it was here that quality proved better than quantity, for the marksmanship, training and discipline of the British troops brought the enemy advance to an abrupt halt.

Other battles followed, at the Aisne, Le Cateau, Nery and elsewhere and by November 1914 the two sides were entrenched along what was to become known as the Western Front, stretching nearly 500 miles, from a point between Nieuport and Dunkirk on the Channel coast to the Vosges Mountains, via Ypres, Vimy, Arras, Rheims and Verdun. The British and Commonwealth troops were concentrated on the northern end of this line in the Flanders, Artois and Somme regions of Northern France.

Very little change took place along this line for the next four years, despite some determined assaults by both sides. The trenches were deeply dug and barbed wire, snipers and machine guns discouraged any movement. Constant shelling coupled with heavy rain turned the countryside into a quagmire; in places the mud was deep enough for a man to drown in it.

It was a war that was to see countless examples of valour by soldiers, sailors and the newly created airmen, regardless of nationality. England in general, and Kent in particular, was not found to be lacking, the county's sons and residents gaining no fewer than nineteen Victoria Crosses.

Lieutenant Philip NEAME

The first Kent Victoria Cross was gained during the early period of this trench warfare by the young Lieutenant Philip Neame. Born at Macknade House, Preston, near Faversham on 12 December 1888, Philip was the youngest child in a family of five boys and one girl. His father, Frederick Neame, was a comfortably off farmer, hop grower and land agent and Philip had a suitably privileged youth. He attended a private school in Westgate and went on to study at the military side at Cheltenham College, as did his father, brothers and cousins. At the age of eighteen he entered the Royal Military Academy, Woolwich and was commissioned into the Royal Engineers as a second lieutenant in July 1908. Promoted full lieutenant in 1910, he served at the School of Military Engineering, Chatham and in Gibraltar. Small and wiry, he had an almost oriental cast of features and quickly demonstrated a gift for planning and organization.

In October 1914 Philip Neame went to France with the 15th Field Company, Royal Engineers and served on the Western Front for the whole of the war. During the First Battle of Ypres, he gained first-hand experience of the inadequacies and paucity of the official British hand grenades and set about creating an alternative. Under his guidance, the Royal Engineers began making home-made devices out of empty jam-tins filled with nails, bits of metal, rivets – anything they could lay their hands on. Two pieces of guncotton and a detonator with a short length of fuse projecting from the end of the tin completed the device.

On 19 November 1914 he was at Neuve Chapelle when the British infantry captured some German trenches, only to be strongly counter attacked by the Germans. Neame and his section were asked by the officer commanding the West Yorkshire Regiment to see if they could help to consolidate the British position with trenches and barbed wire defences so he went off alone to reconnoitre. In one of the forward trenches he came across a party of the West Yorkshires who were under heavy attack from their German counterparts. The officer in charge of the infantry party told Lieutenant Neame that the Germans were throwing grenades or bombs but that his own bombers had all been wounded and the bombs that were left would not go off. A sergeant (who was killed shortly afterwards) asked Neame if he would try some of his jam-tin 'bombs'.

Neame made some enquiries of the wounded bombers and found that they had been unable to light the bombs because they had run out of fuses. Calling upon his experience with these devices, Neame knew he could light them by holding a match-head on the end of the fuse and striking a matchbox across it. Pushing his way to the front of the trench, he began lighting and throwing the bombs into the German trenches, thus holding the trench for forty-five minutes and driving the attack off, even though a machine gun opened up on him every time he stood up on the fire step. He then went out to help the infantrymen to evacuate their wounded back to the previously held British lines, being grazed by rifle bullets twice as he did so. It was for this action that he was awarded the Victoria Cross, being also awarded the Distinguished Service Order in January 1916.

Lieutenant Neame progressed steadily through the ranks, reaching that of temporary lieutenant colonel by the end of the First World War. A crack shot, he won a gold medal in the Running Deer team shooting competition in the 1924 Olympics, being the only man to win both the VC and an Olympic gold medal. Rather less laudably, his 'great passion' was the hunting and killing of big game such as tigers and panthers. In India in 1933 a tigress he had wounded mauled him and he spent two months in hospital with blood poisoning. But even this had a lucky side in that he married the woman who had nursed him during his recovery and they were blessed with three sons and a daughter.

Promoted to major general in 1937, he was the last commandant of the Royal Military College, Woolwich, remaining there until it closed in 1939. By August 1940 he was a temporary lieutenant general, commanding Palestine, Transjordan and Cyprus. The following spring he was the general officer commanding in chief and military governor of Cyrenaica when Rommel began his attack in which the Afrika Corps completely outmanoeuvred and outfought the British troops. During the withdrawal from Benghazi, temporary Lieutenant General Neame was captured by the Germans and handed over to the Italians. Taken to a prison camp near Florence, he was released or escaped in September 1943 following the temporary ousting of Mussolini and reached the advancing Eighth Army and, eventually, returned to England.

Philip Neame was knighted in 1946 and his temporary rank of lieutenant general made substantive. He retired to Kent and died at his home in Selling on 28 April 1978 in his ninetieth year.

Lieutenant George Allan MALING

Although related to the Maling pottery family, George Allan Maling was the son of a general practitioner and followed his father into the medical profession. Born in Sunderland on 6 October 1888, he was educated at Uppingham School and Oxford University before starting his medical training at St Thomas's Hospital. He graduated MB, BCh Oxon in 1914 and the following year took the diplomas MRCS and LRCP.

In January 1915, at the age of twenty-six, he took a temporary commission in the Royal Army Medical Corps and, five months later, went to France on attachment to the 12th Battalion of the Rifle Brigade. On 25 September 1915 the French and British armies began a major offensive that became known as the Battle of Loos, preceded by a four-day artillery barrage. Although General Haig had committed six British divisions to the attack, he had no divisions in reserve and, as soon as the bombardment ceased, the Germans seized the opportunity to bring in their reserves. Although considerable gains were made on the first day, thanks to the covering artillery fire, on the second day the British troops were ordered 'over the top' without the benefit of any covering fire, much to the astonishment of the waiting German machine gunners who inflicted some 50,000 casualties on the vulnerable British men. Eventually the British were forced to order a retreat.

It was as dawn broke on that first day of the battle (25 September) that a group of British Tommies found themselves trapped by heavy artillery fire in and around a ruined house in no man's land, near the village of Fauquissart. Such was the intensity of the German barrage that it was impossible for men from the main body, still in the trenches, to sally forth to aid their comrades. Despite this, hearing that there were literally hundreds of casualties out there, Lieutenant Maling grabbed his medical pack and, with his orderly, ran through the barrage of exploding shells and miraculously arrived at his destination unharmed.

Together with his assistant, Lieutenant Maling moved from casualty to casualty, treating their wounds as best he could and moving some of the less seriously injured men to more sheltered and comfortable positions. Around 11am he was blown down and temporarily stunned by the bursting of a large shell, which wounded his only assistant and killed several of his patients. A second shell shortly afterwards covered him and his instruments in dust and debris but he carried on regardless, now working single-handedly. As night fell the bombardment lessened and he was able to begin moving the wounded to relatively safe places. In all, Lieutenant Maling worked incessantly from dawn on 25 September until around 8am on 26 September, collecting and treating more than 300 casualties in the open and under continuous heavy shell fire. It was for his actions during these two days that Lieutenant Maling was awarded the Victoria Cross.

He continued his duties throughout the war, mainly in France, and rose to the rank of captain. In 1917 he got married and later his wife bore him a son. Following his demobilization at the end of the war he first took a post as resident medical officer at the Victoria Hospital for Children in Chelsea before commencing general practice in Lee, where he was the surgeon to outpatients at St John's Hospital, Lewisham. He died on 9 July 1929 at the very young age of forty and is buried in Chislehurst Cemetery, Kent. His medals are held in the Museum of Army Medical Services, Aldershot.

Sergeant Harry WELLS

Another name associated with the Battle of Loos is that of Sergeant Harry Wells. A true Man of Kent, Harry was born on 19 September 1888 in Herne near Herne Bay and spent all the early years of his tragically short life in that area. On leaving school he became a farm hand, like many of his contemporaries, working at Ridgeway Farm in Herne Bay, where he lost two fingers on his right hand in an accident with a haymaking machine. He then worked for a while at Herne mill before joining the army in 1904 at the age of sixteen, curiously with the Royal Sussex Regiment rather than either of the two Kent regiments or, given his height (over six feet), a Guards regiment.

Harry Wells spent seven years with the regiment, mostly in India, and when he left the army in 1911 he joined the Kent County Constabulary and served as a constable in the Ashford Division. It appears life in the police was not to Harry's liking, however, as he left the force on 31 December 1913. A short spell as a barman at the Beaver Inn, South Ashford, was interrupted by the outbreak of the First World War and Harry Wells was recalled to the Colours, rejoining his old regiment, the Royal Sussex. Given his previous military experience he moved swiftly through the non-commissioned ranks and within a year he was a sergeant.

Like Lieutenant Maling (see previous entry), Sergeant Harry Wells' Victoria Cross was earned during the Battle of Loos, on the same day, 25 September 1915. His platoon was located near Le Routoire Farm and was endeavouring to advance against stubborn enemy resistance when the platoon officer was killed. Sergeant Wells immediately took command and led his men forward to within fifteen yards of the German wire. Nearly half of his platoon were killed or wounded and the survivors were much shaken. With the utmost coolness and bravery, Sergeant Wells rallied them and led them on again. Finally, when very few of his men were left, he stood up and urged them forward once more but, while doing this, he was killed. According to the citation for the award of the medal, 'He gave a magnificent example of courage and determination.'

He was buried in the Dud Corner Cemetery, Loos, Northern France, and his medals are held at the Royal Sussex Regiment Museum in the Redoubt, Eastbourne.

The Reverend William Robert Fountaine ADDISON

William Robert Fountaine's connection with the church would seem to date back to his grandfather, William, who in 1861 was the curate at St Giles' Church, Reading. The Reverend William Addison's eldest son, William Grylls Addison, the father of our hero, was born in or around 1852 but did not follow his father into the church; instead he seems to have made some sort of a living as an 'artist and landscape painter', which is how he was described in the 1891 and 1901 censuses. He seems to have been a more than averagely competent watercolourist but it is not clear just what sort of living he would have made. His works are occasionally sold at auctions today when they fetch £100 to £200 – not a fortune by any standard. Since William Grylls Addison supported a wife and seven children and could afford to employ both a cook and a house parlourmaid, he probably had private, inherited means.

When William Robert Fountaine Addison was born on 13 October 1883 the family were living in Hartley Witney, Hampshire, but in 1896 they moved into Kent and lived at Etching Hill House, Goudhurst, and later in West Terrace, Cranbrook, where his father, the artist, died in 1904. His mother, Alice, was a native of Sevenoaks so perhaps she was the influence that led the family back to her home county. The thirteen-year-old William Robert Fountaine Addison went to Horsmonden village school, so it would seem the family's finances did not stretch to a private education.

The financial situation would have worsened with his father's death and so, at the age of twenty-one, William went to Canada, where he worked for some time on a lumber camp. Later, possibly having earned enough money through hard work to support himself, he returned to England and entered the Salisbury Theological College. He was ordained into the Church of England faith in 1913 and appointed curate of St Edmunds, Salisbury, where in addition to his pastoral work he was able to follow and enjoy his hobby of ornithology. This appointment was to be somewhat short lived as, with the outbreak of war, the peace-loving priest evidently felt he had to do his bit in the great struggle against Germany and so, in September 1915, he joined the Army Chaplains Department as a temporary chaplain to the Forces, fourth class.

Although mental images of the First World War conjure up the dreadful scenes in the trenches on the Western Front, the war was being prosecuted in other theatres, not least of which was Mesopotamia (present-day Iraq). Here, a combined Anglo-Indian force was battling, somewhat vainly, against determined, well-trained and ferocious Turkish troops. Frontal attacks by the 13th Division against prepared positions on the north bank of the Tigris River resulted in 2,800 casualties without any progress being made. There was a little more success at Beit Ayeesa on the south bank but the Turks drove the 3rd Division back with 1,150 casualties. A further attempt, made at Sanna-i-Yat by the 7th Division in atrocious weather, also failed, but it was here that Chaplain Addison distinguished himself. With heavy casualties all around, many lying exposed to withering enemy fire, he ignored the danger to himself and went out and brought a wounded man back to the comparative safety of the British trenches. He then went out again and, subjected to heavy rifle and machine gun fire, tended several more by bandaging their wounds before escorting them back to safety. In addition to these unaided efforts, his example and utter disregard for his own safety encouraged the nervous stretcher bearers to go forward and collect the wounded despite the enemy fire. For this courageous example he was awarded the Victoria Cross.

The Reverend Addison remained in the Army Chaplains Department after the Armistice and served in several posts in England, the Sudan, Malta and with the Shanghai Defence Force. He retired from the army in 1938, having served for more than twenty years and lived in twenty-one different houses. When the Second World War broke out in 1939 Addison was reappointed chaplain to the forces and became deputy assistant chaplain general in South Wales.

The Reverend William Robert Fountain Addison, VC died at St Leonards-on-Sea on 7 January 1962, his funeral taking place at St Barnabas Church, Bexhill-on-Sea, followed by interment at Brookwood Cemetery, near Woking. His Victoria Cross is on display at the National Army Museum in London.

Acting Corporal William Richard COTTER

William Richard Cotter was registered as being born in Folkestone in 1882 (or 1883), the son of Richard and Amy Cotter (née Richards). Richard was an Irishman from Cork, working as a plasterer's labourer in the Folkestone area, but Amy was a Maid of Kent, born in Barham in 1860. In 1881 the couple were living at Mill Yard Cottage, Horn Street, Cheriton but by 1891 their address was 43 Walton Road, Folkestone, so it is assumed that they moved from Cheriton to Folkestone just before Richard was born.

Richard was the eldest of six children to be born to Richard and Amy and there is no doubt the family found it hard to survive on Richard's meagre wages as a labourer. The prospects for a poorly educated son of lower-working-class parents would have been very limited and so it is not surprising that, having left school at the age of thirteen, William could only follow in his father's footsteps and work as a casual labourer.

Perhaps inspired by tales of derring-do in South Africa, or perhaps merely seeking a better life, William joined the 3rd (Militia) Battalion of The Buffs (East Kent Regiment) around the turn of the century and, apparently enjoying (part-time) army life, he enlisted in the regular army in October 1901. Describing himself on the enlistment form as 'still serving' because of his position in the Militia (i.e. Territorials), he was duly taken on for seven years with the colours and five years in the reserve (described as 'Short Service') and posted to one of the regular battalions, either the 1st or the 2nd.

William Cotter had completed his seven-year engagement and would have nearly completed his reserve commitment when mobilization began in anticipation of war around 1913–1914. Recalled to the colours, he reported to the regimental depot at Canterbury. Despite the fact that he had lost an eye in an incident some years previously when he was 'glassed' in a fight in Dover, William Cotter was one of the handful of experienced soldiers selected to form the nucleus of a new battalion, the 6th (Service) Battalion. This was one of the first units to arrive in France and see combat in the trenches. With only a couple of brief exceptions, Lance Corporal Cotter served in the front line for the next eighteen months, often in the thick of things, and distinguished himself in close-quarter fighting and bayonet charges.

During the autumn of 1915, major battles had been waging around the Hohenzollern Redoubt, a formidable German fortification near Auchy-les-Mines in France. Although the main assault had run out of steam by the following spring, there was still a lot of fighting in the area and it was in the course of a further attack on 6 March 1916 that Acting Corporal Cotter was severely wounded. His right leg had been blown off at the knee and he had been wounded in both arms. Despite these dreadful wounds, and in agonizing pain, he crawled unaided to a crater fifty yards away where a group of his men were resisting the German onslaught. In the absence of any officer or more senior NCO, Corporal Cotter took command, steadying the nervous men and controlling their fire. He issued the necessary orders and altered the dispositions of his men, cheering them on when they had to meet a fresh counter attack by the enemy. This little band held on to their precarious position for two hours, against heavy odds. Only when the attack had abated did he allow his wounds to be roughly dressed, after which he had to wait a further, and no doubt crucial, fourteen hours before he could be evacuated to the rear for proper medical treatment. Despite the obvious pain and loss of blood he continued to have a cheery word for all who passed by. His magnificent courage helped greatly to save a critical situation.

There is no doubt that it was the severity of Cotter's wounds and the considerable loss of blood he had suffered due to the delay in getting proper treatment that led to this brave man succumbing a week later in hospital. On 14 March 1916, Acting Corporal William Richard Cotter died of his wounds and was buried in the Lillers Communal Cemetery, the only 'Buff' to win the Victoria Cross in the First World War. He was thirty-three years of age. It appears that his father predeceased him as his next of kin in 1916 was shown as his mother, Amy Cotter, who was then living at 2 Barton Cottages,

Sandgate, Kent. His medals are held by the National Army Museum in London.

A picture exists showing Corporal Cotter in dress uniform and wearing the Victoria Cross, but since the medal was awarded posthumously it is assumed that this is an 'imagined' likeness made by an artist after the event, or an existing picture or photograph which has been altered by the addition of the medal.

Lieutenant Richard Basil Brandram JONES

Richard Jones was born at 7 Honor Oak Rise, Anerley, Bromley, Kent on 30 April 1897, the only son of Henry Thomas Brandram Jones and Caroline Jones. Henry Jones was a white lead manufacturer and would seem to have been quite successful as he could afford to send his son to Dulwich College from 1909 to 1914.

There was little time for young Richard to contemplate his future, whether this should be in his father's business or elsewhere, since the declaration of war in the same year that he left school meant that any plans, ambitions and dreams had to be put to one side while the young men of the country put on uniform and went to fight for their country.

Thanks to his education and background, Richard was granted a commission in the 8th Battalion of the Loyal North Lancashire Regiment and soon found himself in the thick of things on the Western Front. Trench warfare was still being waged, with the life expectancy of a junior officer being measured in days rather than months. Frequent sorties were made 'over the top' in an endeavour to drive the enemy from their entrenched positions, but these were usually abortive and always involved great loss of life.

Sometimes the attacking units were content to occupy a shell crater (of which there were very many) from which to harry the Germans and it was in just such a position that Temporary Lieutenant Richard Jones found himself on 21 May 1916. Leading his platoon across no man's land, he succeeded in driving away some German soldiers who were occupying a large crater near Vimy and took up occupation in their stead. This small band managed to hold off sporadic attempts by the enemy to regain the position but, around 7.30pm, a large mine was detonated forty yards from the crater, followed immediately by a heavy artillery barrage aimed at the British trenches, thus isolating Lieutenant Jones and his men from their comrades. The barrage was swiftly followed by an attack by an overwhelming number of German infantrymen. Lieutenant Jones encouraged his fearful platoon and, to set an example, installed himself on the lip of the crater and set about firing his revolver at the advancing hordes. At least fifteen of the enemy were accounted for in this way, with Lieutenant Jones counting them off out loud as he did so in order to encourage his men, who were thus inspired by his example to put up a stout defence of their precarious position.

Finally, Lieutenant Jones's ammunition ran out but, undeterred, he took up a hand grenade to throw at the enemy. However, as he reached the edge of the crater, a bullet took him in the head and he died instantly, before he even had time to throw his grenade. Although dismayed by the loss of their officer, the members of the platoon remained sufficiently inspired to continue the battle and, when their ammunition was exhausted, they began to throw stones and ammunition boxes at the enemy until only nine men were left and these tattered remnants had no alternative but to retire and make their way back to their own lines.

Lieutenant Richard Basil Brandram Jones, aged just nineteen, was awarded a posthumous Victoria Cross for his conspicuous courage and inspiring leadership. His remains were never recovered and he is listed as having 'no known grave' on the memorial at the Faubourg d'Amiens cemetery, Arras. His medal is privately owned.

Like a number of other VC holders, he is pictured wearing his medal on a cigarette card, but this has obviously been 'doctored' as he never lived to wear this symbol of courage.

Captain Thomas Riversdale COLYER-FERGUSSON

Thomas Riversdale Colyer-Fergusson and his brothers were descended from distinguished Kentish families, as evidenced by his somewhat unusual combination of names. The Fergusson part is fairly straightforward, being the ancient surname handed down on the male side. The Irish name Riversdale he owes to his maternal grandmother, the daughter of one Riversdale Grenfell who, in turn, was descended from a Lady Riversdale. The Colyer part of the surname comes from his paternal grandmother, Mary Ann Somes, wife of Sir James R Fergusson who lived at Hever Court, near Gravesend. Mary Ann's father was Thomas Colyer of Wombwell Hall, near Northfleet. This latter property was eventually inherited by Thomas Riversdale's father, Sir Thomas Colyer Colyer-Fergusson, who not only took the name Colyer as his second forename but also added it to his surname.

Sir Thomas Colyer Colyer-Fergusson and his wife, Beatrice Stanley, married in 1890 and had three sons, all of whom served in the army during the First World War: Max Christian, William Porteous and Thomas Riversdale. Only Thomas failed to return.

Thomas, the youngest son, was born at 13 Lower Berkley Street, Portman Square, London on 18 February 1896 and was baptized in Southfleet, suggesting that his mother had gone to the family home in Northfleet for the confinement. But Sir Thomas had, in 1889, the year prior to his marriage, bought Ightham Mote, near Sevenoaks, which complemented his inherited ownership of Wombwell Hall and was to be the main family home for the foreseeable future. At the time of purchase, Ightham Mote was in a rather sorry state, and Sir Thomas spent a lot of time and money on repairing it. He owned this property and resided there until his death in 1951. Sir Thomas is also recorded as occupying Wombwell Hall in 1909 and so it would appear that he owned and used both premises for at least part of his lifetime.

With such a privileged background, it will come as no surprise to learn that Thomas Riversdale Colyer-Fergusson was educated at Harrow School and (briefly) Oriel College, Oxford. His great passion was sport and, in particular, hunting with the West Kent Hounds. In September 1914, at the age of eighteen and when the First World War was but a month old, he joined the Public Schools Battalion and on 20 February 1915 he was granted a temporary commission in the Northamptonshire Regiment. This commission was made substantive later the same year. In July 1916 he was wounded in the right arm at Contalmaison and was appointed acting captain in January 1917 whilst serving with the 2nd Battalion of his regiment.

On 31 July 1917 the regiment was involved in what became known as the Battle of Pilckem Ridge. It succeeded in taking Bellewaarde Lake with the use of mortars firing thermite bombs and went on to take the Ridge. The battalion's commanding officer, Lieutenant Colonel Christopher Buckle (aged 29!), who was himself wounded by a shell that day, later wrote to Captain Colyer-Fergusson's family in the following terms:

> In this last attack I selected his company for the most difficult portion of trench within the battalion objective. He carried out his task most brilliantly. For the capture of a certain line of German trenches, his

company had to follow our barrage through a very broken wood, which proved to be full of [barbed] wire. He soon saw that it would be impossible to keep his whole company up with the barrage for the final assault, and if he failed to keep up with it he would probably fail to capture the trench, so he picked out ten or a dozen men and with them pushed on ahead, and without any further assistance, captured his portion of the German trench. Almost as soon as he got in he perceived a company of Germans advancing against him in mass formation and a bare hundred yards away. He and his picked men knocked out twenty or thirty of them with rifle fire, and the remainder of them surrendered as the rest of his company came up. He came and reported to me in the same trench about half an hour later, when I got up to him. Five minutes later he was shot through the forehead by a German machine gun bullet. I think his death was more deeply felt in the regiment than any other I have known. To my mind he was the most promising officer under my command. I cannot hope ever to be able to replace him he, besides being a first rate officer, being such a thorough sportsman and the cheeriest of companions.

A staff officer at the 8th Division headquarters added:

he behaved with quite exceptional gallantry … and set an example which everybody in the division is proud of. Not only did he display exceptional gallantry, but also sound military knowledge and tactical insight far beyond his years, and … enabled us to secure all objectives which would have cost many lives but for his prompt and gallant action.

In fact, according to the citation for the award of the Victoria Cross, published in the *London Gazette* on 6 September 1917, the details were not quite as outlined by Colonel Buckle. Captain Colyer-Fergusson was accompanied by just six men, including his platoon sergeant, William Boulding, a recalled reservist from Dartford who was awarded the Distinguished Conduct Medal for his part in the action. During the action, accompanied only by his orderly, Private Basil Ellis (who also received the DCM), Captain Colyer-Fergusson attacked and captured an enemy machine gun and turned it on the attackers, many of whom were killed and a large number were driven into the hands of an adjoining British unit. Later, assisted by just his sergeant, he again attacked and captured a second enemy machine gun; by that time he had been joined by other portions of his company and was able to consolidate his position. 'The conduct of this officer throughout forms an amazing record of dash, gallantry and skill, for which no reward can be too great having regard to the importance of the position won. This gallant officer was shortly afterwards killed by a sniper.'

A brother officer, offering his condolences to the Colyer-Fergusson family, described how the manner and circumstances of 'Riv's' death were a great comfort to him as 'he died in the best of spirits in the very moment of success, and a success that was rendered possible by his own brave action. No man could wish for a finer and more manly ending to this life, God grant, when my time comes, I may meet it in like manner.'

Captain Thomas Riversdale Colyer-Fergusson VC was just twenty-one when he died, a brave and promising young life cruelly cut short, like so many in that 'war to end all wars'. He lies in the Menin Road South Military Cemetery in Ypres, Belgium and his Victoria Cross is on display in the museum of the Northamptonshire Regiment in Northampton. His brother William Porteous Colyer-Fergusson also served in the Northamptonshire Regiment and was wounded in 1917 but he and his other brother, Max Christian Colyer-Fergusson of the RASC, both survived the war.

As mentioned earlier, the father of these three brothers, Sir Thomas Colyer Colyer-Fergusson, owned and lived in Ightham Mote until his death in 1951. His grandson, the thirty-five-year-old Sir James Herbert Hamilton Colyer-Fergusson, the son of the late Max Christian Hamilton Colyer-Fergusson, inherited Ightham Mote but promptly sold the contents by public auction. The bare house was bought by a group of local enthusiasts who proposed to restore this very ancient manor house to its former glory but the task proved too great and too expensive for them and so, after two years, the property was sold on to an American from Maine, Mr Charles Henry Robinson, who spent a lot of money on the building. On his death in 1985 the property was left to the National Trust which, in turn, has spent some millions of pounds on a definitive restoration of this lovely old building, parts of which date back to the fourteenth century.

Major Alexander Malins LAFONE

Another Victoria Cross that was won during 1917 other than on the Western Front was that awarded to Major Alexander Malins Lafone of the Middlesex Yeomanry for his deeds in what was then known as Palestine.

Alexander Lafone was born in Lancashire in 1870, the son of Henry Lafone, a wharfinger (i.e. someone who owns or runs a wharf) of some social standing, and his wife, Lucy. By the time Alexander was eleven, the Lafone household – consisting of Henry and his wife, Alexander, his older brother Henry and his four sisters, plus three domestic servants – had moved south to London and were living in Elmsharde, Camberwell. Alexander was enrolled at Dulwich College, where he continued to be educated for the next eight years. On leaving school he studied engineering and worked for a firm in Gainsborough before going out to Assam as an assistant manager on a tea plantation in 1894. After three years in India he returned to England to live at the current family home, Phoenix House, Alleyn Park, Camberwell, and began work in his father's firm on Butler's Wharf.

Around the turn of the century the Lafone family moved into Kent and took up residence at Court Lodge, Knockholt where Henry Lafone and his wife continued to live until their death, when they were buried in the village churchyard.

At some point Alexander Lafone joined the 1st County of London (Middlesex) Yeomanry (a predecessor of the Territorial Army) but was seconded, as a sergeant, to the 49th Company of the Imperial Yeomanry (Montgomeryshire) on the outbreak of the Second Boer War. This unit (and several others like it) had been raised from the Yeomanry specifically to serve as mounted infantry in South Africa. The initial engagement was for one year, the officers and men to provide their own horse, saddlery, clothing and accoutrements. Dress was to be plain coloured Norfolk jackets, breeches and gaiters with a felt hat. Arms, ammunition and camping gear would be supplied by the army.

Alexander Lafone was wounded in the face during the course of his second engagement and was invalided out in 1901, by which time he was serving as a Lieutenant in the Hertfordshire Yeomanry. He stayed on in Africa, working for the Colonial Office as an Assistant Resident in Northern Nigeria, but recurrent bouts of fever forced him to return to England where he returned to his shipping career, still maintaining his links with the Yeomanry or Militia.

By the time the First World War broke out in August 1914, Alexander Lafone was a major in his original unit, the 1st County of London (Middlesex) Yeomanry. Major 'Laffy' Lafone was exceptionally proud and fond of his men and was regarded by them with respectful affection. He was noted for his rather dry sense of humour and for his peculiar mannerism of fidgeting with his tie – said to be a habit he shared with the Prince of Wales.

When the regiment was mobilized and eventually sent to Egypt as part of the 8th (London) Mounted Brigade, Major Lafone took command of B Squadron. He saw action in the Sinai Desert and then took part in the great advance on Palestine in 1917, during which this forty-seven-year-old officer was to gain the Victoria Cross and lose his life.

With the completion of the rail link and water pipeline from Tel el Fara to Karm, the latter township provided a very valuable supply centre and source of water for the troops in this desert area and was a serious threat to the Turkish defensive positions. The final logistic preparations for the battle for Turk-held Beersheba was complete and to protect this vital supply depot from the Ottoman forces at Abu Hareira it was decided to transform an existing ring of temporary outposts into a permanent defensive line. To this end it was ordered that the outpost line be occupied and converted into its permanent role.

The Middlesex Yeomanry was to occupy one of a number of cavalry outposts, with the 3rd County of London Yeomanry (The Sharpshooters) on the left flank and the 1st City of London Yeomanry (The Roughriders) on the right. This particular outpost ran along the El Buggar ridge, a high ridge of loose sand and sandstone which overlooked the enemy positions. The key positions on the ridge were two rising hills, known as points 630 and 720; three troops from C Squadron, commanded by the monocle-wearing Captain McDougall, held Point 630 and the dismounted B Squadron, under Major 'Laffy' Lafone, was sited on Point 720, with A Squadron patrolling the space between these high points. The regimental headquarters were sited some three miles back with which the only means of communication was by heliograph by day and lamp by night.

Point 720 was a cone-shaped hill with a small ruined house on the summit. There were two shallow rifle pits to the right of the house, a small trench on the left flank and a slightly deeper, cruciform trench about a hundred yards to the rear. Two troops from B Squadron occupied the trenches and a strong piquet held the flank. A further troop was used as a standing patrol about a mile to the rear. The atmosphere was fairly relaxed as the regiment had carried out similar duties in the past without there being any serious trouble with the enemy. But this time it was going to be different.

Soon after the troops were 'stood to' at 3am on 27 October 1917, it became apparent that B and C Squadrons were under serious attack. A Royal Flying Corps reconnaissance plane estimated the attacking force as being 3–5,000 strong with two regiments of cavalry and several battalions of infantry. Their objective was clearly to destroy the railhead and so slow General Allenby's advance on Beersheba.

The first attack was on Point 630 and those on Point 720 were initially astonished to see flares going up on the adjacent hill but their surprise quickly turned to concern when they could discern in the half-light large bodies of horsemen charging towards them. B Squadron immediately opened fire from their entrenched positions and caused the horsemen to withdraw, and another assault by a contingent of Turkish cavalry that had somehow ridden round to the rear of the position was similarly dealt with and received a hot reception from the troopers in the cruciform trench. The attacking force, consisting of 1,200 men from the Ottoman 3rd Cavalry Division and a battalion from the 27th Infantry Division, failed to take the Point.

As the day gradually grew lighter, B Squadron could see a large body of Turkish infantry massing for an attack which they soon launched, attempting to overrun the hill by a bayonet charge. They proved an easy target for the British riflemen, who picked them off by the dozen. Major Lafone was very much 'hands on' and was firing his rifle as fast as he could, calling out his score all the while: 'Eight, nine, ten – missed him – eleven …' Unable to complete their assault, the Turks brought in a squadron of Turkish lancers, but they too were mown down by the concentrated rifle fire and that from the Yeomanry squadron's Hotchkiss machine gun. Corporal Rangecroft, the squadron's machine gunner, swept off a line of about thirty lancers, shouting 'That's the stuff to give them!'

Again and again the enemy renewed their assault with both infantry and cavalry but were continually repulsed. At one point they left fifteen casualties within twenty yards of the trenches before being beaten back, one man being bayoneted by Major Lafone himself. Frustrated, the Turks brought up their artillery and began a bombardment of Point 620, shelling the trenches and the ruined house. A sergeant who, at great risk, had managed to ride back to the regimental headquarters returned at 7.30am with a message that Major Lafone was to hold on.

Eventually the right flank on Point 720 was driven in, leaving B Squadron's main garrison unprotected on that side, and as the firing line developed the whole hill was swept by rifle and machine gun fire from about 2,000 enemy troops. Such was the ferocity of the assault that anyone who was unable to shelter in one of the shallow trenches quickly became a casualty.

Lieutenant Van den Bergen, with nearly all his troop killed or wounded, showed great courage in his defence of the stone house but was soon mortally wounded and died, saying with a wistful smile, 'Give my love to my mother.' Lieutenant Stuart hastened to take his place but he too was soon wounded and Major Lafone, on hearing the news, ran to the rifle pits by the stone house. He now sent his last message back to his headquarters: 'My casualties are heavy, six stretchers required. I shall hold on to the last, as I cannot get my wounded away.' Faced with making a heroic and desperate last stand, he constantly cheered on his surviving men, telling them, 'The infantry will soon be up,' but anyone looking to the rear would not see any signs of movement on the desert plain. The remaining water was given to the huddled wounded men and, as the sun rose higher, all were suffering the pangs of intense thirst. By now the number of wounded was so great that it was difficult for the defenders to move and continue shooting so Major Lafone ordered those wounded who were able to walk to move to a trench further back so as to leave the forward trenches free for those who were continuing with the defence.

A body of enemy cavalry made its way round the exposed flank and attacked the waiting led horses which had already come under fire earlier in the day, resulting in every man having charge of about ten horses. Squadron Sergeant Major Dixon, in charge of the led horse contingent, managed to get a Hotchkiss machine gun into action and beat off the attack. Sadly, most of the horses were waiting for riders who would never return for, around 11am, under cover of artillery and machine gun fire, the Turks launched a final assault on the stone house. All the occupants were wounded men but, despite their wounds, under 'Laffy' Lafone's encouragement they fought to the bitter end. As the enemy came ever closer, Major Lafone marched out into the open, firing point-blank from the shoulder, and, at twenty yards, beat back this last attack, only to fall grievously wounded. His last words to his sergeant were: 'I wonder if there is any chance of the infantry getting up in time?'

Undeterred, the little garrison fought on until there were only three unwounded survivors who, helping as many of the wounded as possible, made a dash for safety. Looking over their shoulder they could see the Turkish cavalry sweep over the hill, but the post had been held to the bitter

end and long enough to render its capture useless to the enemy who had
left more than 200 of their number dead on the slopes of the hill. The
Yeomanry had held the point for some seven hours against overwhelming
odds and succeeded in denying it to the attacking forces long enough to
prevent the enemy from achieving his intention and possibly digging in on
the position. Had the enemy done so, he could have rendered work on the
railway impossible and would have been extremely difficult to dislodge. As
it was, the determined defence of the El Buggar Ridge gave the supporting
British infantry and other reinforcements time to move up and retake the
ridge without opposition.

Major Alexander Malins Lafone's father died in the same year as his
brave son and his mother also around this time. He never married and so his
Victoria Cross was presented to his elder brother, Henry, the archdeacon
at Grange-over-Sands. It is now held by his old school, Dulwich College.
Major Lafone is buried in Beersheba Military Cemetery, Israel, and is
also commemorated on his parents' grave in the graveyard at Knockholt
Church.

Lieutenant Colonel Arthur Drummond BORTON

Continuing the series of Victoria Crosses won in the Middle East in 1917, we
come to Lieutenant Colonel Arthur Drummond Borton, who rejoiced in the
soubriquet of 'Bosky'. He was a member of a long-standing Kentish family
whose family seat was Cheveney, Yalding. There is some question as to where
Arthur Drummond Borton was born on 1 July 1883: most references quote
Cheveney but some census returns give Malta. Both are distinct possibilities
since 'Bosky's' grandfather, General Sir Arthur Borton, was the Governor
of Malta and his father, Irish-born Arthur Close Borton, was an officer in
the 13th (Somerset) Light Infantry and acted as the general's aide-de-camp.
Whichever is correct, it is reasonable to include Arthur as a native of, or
resident in, Kent and thereby qualified for inclusion in this book.

Arthur's father travelled around the country in accordance with his
postings. In 1871 he was an ensign at Pembroke Dock; in 1891 a thirty-nine-
year-old major living with his family at Trull, Somerset, having married
Adelaide Beatrice in Bromley in 1880. By this time (1891) Arthur was
seven years of age and had a brother, Amyas, four years old and a baby sister,
Dorothea, just ten months. The household comprised a governess, no fewer
than *seven* household servants (of whom three came from Kent, presumably

having been previously engaged at Cheveney) and Private John Foot, the major's batman or 'servant'.

As soon as he was old enough, Arthur 'Bosky' Borton was packed off to Eton College where he completed his education, entering the Royal Military College, Sandhurst in 1900. He was commissioned into the 60th Rifles (King's Royal Rifle Corps) in 1902 and saw service in South Africa. In 1906 he was promoted to lieutenant but, shortly afterwards, bored with inaction in India and a shortage of cash (or perhaps through ill health), he resigned his commission and returned to England before going off to seek his fortune in the United States of America where he tried his hand at fruit farming, no doubt drawing on his experience in the 'Garden of England'. His involvement in various hare-brained schemes, such as the purchase of a lake in order to sell the ice in the winter and the invention of a new kind of bottle-stopper, were all doomed to failure and his repeated demands on his father for financial support led to a serious deterioration in their relationship. Occasionally forced to sleep in a park and to forego food for lack of funds, coupled with an increasing dependence on alcohol, 'Bosky' Borton was rapidly becoming an archetypal 'black sheep of the family'.

However, with the outbreak of war in 1914, the thirty-one-year-old former soldier returned to England determined to 'do his bit' and on 22 October 1914 re-enlisted in his old regiment, the KRRC. Before long, however, Lieutenant Borton transferred to the newly formed Royal Flying Corps and joined his younger brother, Amyas 'Biffy' Borton, as an observer before leaving for France with No 3 Squadron RFC in January 1915. Only two months later he was involved in a serious flying accident, resulting in him breaking or dislocating his neck, and Lieutenant Arthur 'Bosky' Borton was invalided out of the service. He returned to Cheveney to convalesce and was shortly joined by his brother, who had received a terrible facial wound in the course of a dogfight. A bullet had entered his neck, passed below his tongue before exiting via the left jaw bone but, despite this, he had succeed in flying twenty miles back to the British lines before landing. 'Biffy' was recommended for the Victoria Cross but was given the DSO instead.

It is hard to keep a good man down and Arthur Borton was undoubtedly a determined one. The ink had hardly dried on his discharge papers before he had joined the Royal Naval Volunteer Reserve (RNVR) and, as a lieutenant commander, was on his way to Gallipoli! At first sight it would seem curious to appoint a military man as a naval officer but this becomes clearer when one notes that he was placed in charge of two squadrons of Motor Machine Gun Armoured Cars belonging to the Royal Naval Air Service, with which he took part in the Suvla Bay landings on 7 August 1915. These landings were not a great success and Lieutenant Commander Borton, in deep despair at the inept leadership and the quality of the inexperienced volunteers who comprised the landing force, wrote, 'as compared to the Turks, we are nothing but a bunch of amiable amateurs when it comes to scrapping in this kind of country'. Finally, in December 1915, the whole force was evacuated from Suvla with 'Bosky's' Naval Battery providing the covering fire, being among the last to leave.

On his return to England, Lieutenant Commander Arthur Borton, RNVR was awarded the Distinguished Service Order (DSO) 'In recognition of most valuable services whilst in command of a detachment of Royal Marine Motor Machine Guns in difficult and dangerous parts of the line on the Gallipoli Peninsular.' (There has been considerable discussion by Great War enthusiasts as to whether the reference to the 'Royal Marines' was, in fact, an error.)

Once again there was a change of service and rank when, in June 1916, he once more (the third time!) joined the army, being promoted to major and appointed second in command of the 2/22nd Battalion, The London Regiment (The Queen's). He was soon with his new regiment in France but in November 1916 it was sent to Salonika (Greece) where he eventually became its commanding officer and was promoted to lieutenant colonel – something he regarded as a great honour.

From Salonika the regiment moved to the Palestine theatre, via Egypt, where the two brothers were briefly reunited. Here, two attempts to capture Gaza had failed, and General Edmund Allenby had been sent from France to take charge of the offensive. The British and Australian troops were superior both in quantity and quality but the Turks were in a virtually unassailable position, although they were weak on their left (east) flank at Beersheba. However, the lack of water on this approach led them to believe it would be impossible to mount an attack from here. The British therefore embarked on a massive programme of transporting water and reopening wells destroyed by the enemy in order to support a covert attack on Beersheba, all the time endeavouring to convince the Turks that the main assault would be, as expected, on Gaza. The ruse was a complete success and Beersheba was taken with few casualties.

Further successes followed, not without heavy losses on both sides, and the Gaza–Beersheba line was looking vulnerable when the British mounted an attack on a broad front near Sheria, around the centre of the Turkish line. On the morning of 7 November 1917 the major assault on Gaza was launched, during which the 60th Division, including The Queens, attacked the strong Turkish position on the hill of Tel-el-Sheria.

Lieutenant Colonel 'Bosky' Borton deployed his battalion ready for the attack and, at dawn, led his troops against strong opposition. When the leading waves were checked by withering fire he showed utter contempt for danger and moved freely up and down the line despite heavy fire and then led his men forward, capturing the position. At a later stage in the fight he led a party of volunteers against a battery of field guns in action at point-blank range, capturing the guns and the detachments. His fearless leadership was an inspiring example to the whole brigade and earned him the coveted Victoria Cross.

These bare facts, as provided in the citation for the award, are embellished by the contents of a letter 'Bosky' wrote to his father after the event:

> we were in a devilish awkward fix – we were swept by machine gun fire from both flanks and behind their artillery put down a barrage on top of us and if it had not been that the light was so bad – would have been wiped out in a matter of minutes. It was impossible to stay where we were and hopeless to go back and so to go forward was the only thing to do. And we went!
>
> One of the men had a football. How it came to be there goodness knows. Anyway we kicked off and rushed the first guns, dribbling the ball with us. I take it the Turk thought we were dangerous lunatics but we stopped for nothing, not even to shoot, and the bayonet had its day. For 3000 yards, we swept up everything, finally capturing a field battery and its entire gun crews. The battery fired its last round at us at 25 yards … I hope it may mean a bar [to the DSO].

Instead, Lieutenant Colonel Arthur Drummond 'Bosky' Borton, DSO gained the ultimate award – the Victoria Cross.

The action was supported in the air by 'Biffy' Borton's wing and his description, based on information gained from others on the ground, was more colourful:

Bosky called for ten volunteers and went straight for the guns, which opened fire at 150 yards, with their fuses set at zero! They killed or captured the whole of their crews and ... the last gun fired when they were 10 yards from the guns and the man who pulled the string immediately flung up his hands and said in a broad German accent, 'I vas an Arab!' to which a voice at 'Bosky's' elbow replied, 'Arab be ... ed!' and a bayonet disappeared in the region of the third button of the 'Arab's' coat. Bosky, meanwhile, armed to the teeth with a walking stick and a stream of blasphemy (I should have said 'armed to the gums' as according to one account, he mislaid his teeth, so luckily no one knew what he was saying.)

Lieutenant Colonel Arthur Borton received a great reception in his home village of Yalding in February 1918 before he and his wife went to Buckingham Palace to collect both the VC and the DSO from the King. He returned to the Middle East as an acting brigadier and, after the Armistice, went on to serve in the North Russian Campaign of 1919 and was one of the pall bearers at the Burial of the Unknown Warrior on 11 November 1920.

Life after the war for 'Bosky' Borton was not a happy one. He flitted from one job to another and began to drink heavily, a situation that prompted his father to change his will, denying him the family residence at Cheveney – something Arthur took very badly. With his wife, Lorna, whom he had married in 1915, he went to live at 3 Park Lane, Southwold, Suffolk , living on private means, and it was here that he died from a stroke on 5 January 1933, at the age of fifty. His body was returned to Cheveney and was buried in Hunton parish burial ground. The army provided a guard of honour and two buglers to sound the Last Post and Reveille.

'Bosky' Borton's father, Lieutenant Colonel Arthur Close Borton, DL JP was living in retirement at Cheveney when the First World War began but volunteered for the civilian Volunteer Training Corps – the forerunner of the Second World War Home Guard – and was appointed in command of what was to become the 2nd (Volunteer) Battalion of the Queen's Own Royal West Kent Regiment. He died in 1927 in Maidstone. His second son, Amyas 'Biffy' Borton, inherited the family home at Cheveney, having served with distinction in the Black Watch, the Royal Flying Corps and Royal Air Force, retiring as Air Vice Marshal Amyas Borton, DSO. The last Borton, he died in 1969, after which Cheveney passed out of the family.

It was reported in 2010 that Arthur Borton's grave in Hunton had been sadly neglected and a few First World War enthusiasts made some efforts to tidy it up, deploring the fact that the local residents had not taken greater care of the last resting place of their local hero.

Lieutenant Colonel Christopher BUSHELL

Christopher Bushell was born in Cheshire on 31 October 1888 and came from a wealthy wine importing family, his grandfather having amassed a fortune through the business he set up in Liverpool in the mid 1800s. Christopher's father, Reginald, was in due course made a partner in the business and when he died in 1904 his widow, Caroline, acquired property in the Knightsbridge area of London and another at St Margaret's-at-Cliffe, near Dover, which became home to young Christopher.

Not that he saw too much of this delightful village overlooking the Straits of Dover: after attending Moorland School, Heswall until 1900, he went on to Rugby School at the age of thirteen where he became good friends with Rupert Brooke, who was to become famous as the short-lived soldier poet ('The Old Vicarage', 'Grantchester', 'The Soldier'). From Rugby, Christopher Bushell went to Corpus Christi College, Oxford, to read law, graduating in 1909.

On leaving Oxford, Christopher took a job with a firm of solicitors in Liverpool before entering the Inner Temple, London, as a student barrister with chambers at 2 New Square, Lincolns Inn. During this time he stayed at his mother's Knightsbridge home. He was called to the bar in November 1911 but soon found that life as a barrister was not sufficiently exciting and joined the British Army Special Reserve of Officers in 1912 as a second lieutenant in the 1st Battalion, Queen's (Royal West Surrey) Regiment.

When war broke out in August 1914 the battalion was mobilized and arrived at Zeebrugge as part of the BEF in early October to be almost immediately involved in the Battle of Mons. By 1 November 1914, during the First Battle of Ypres, there were only thirty-two survivors of the original battalion. Reinforced and reconstituted, the 1st Battalion took part in the battles of Loos (1915) and the Somme (1916).

During a brief spell of home leave in August 1915, Christopher Bushell took the opportunity to marry his fiancée, Rachel Lambert, at the Church of St Gregory and St Martin in Wye, Rachel's father having formerly been the rector of Wye church. The union was blessed a year later by the birth of a daughter, Elizabeth Hope Bushell, who was born in Wye.

1. Sergeant Major Charles Wooden, VC.

2. Charge of the Light Brigade.

3. The Light Brigade VCs.

4. The Battle of Inkerman.

5. The Siege of Sebastopol.

6. Captain MC Dixon, VC.

7. The Battle of Rangiriri, 1863.

8. Major William Leet, VC.

9. Private Thomas Byrne, VC.

10. The Charge of the 21st Lancers at Omdurman.

11. Captain JD Grant, VC.

12. Boer Commandos.

13. Artist's impression of Trooper J Doogan's rescue of Major Brownlow.

14. Artist's impression of Second Lieutenant Norwood's rescue of a fallen trooper.

15. Lieutenant HEM Douglas, VC.

16. Captain WN Congreve, VC.

17. Lieutenant FN Parsons, VC.

18. Corporal FH Kirby, VC.

19. Private W House, VC.

20. Trench warfare – The Somme, 1916.

21. Sergeant WB Traynor, VC.

22. Lieutenant P Neame, VC.

23. Lieutenant GA Maling, VC.

24. Sergeant H Wells, VC.

25. The Reverend WRF Addison, VC.

26. Corporal W Cotter, VC.

27. Lieutenant RBB Jones, VC.

28. Major AM Lafone, VC.

29. Lieutenant Colonel AD Borton, VC.

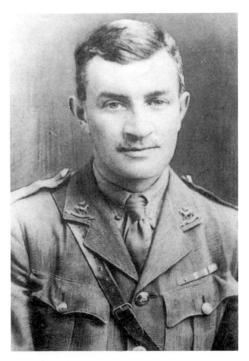

30. Lieutenant Colonel C Bushell, VC.

31. Lieutenant CH Sewell, VC.

32. Lieutenant DJ Dean, VC.

33. Captain RN Stuart, VC.

34. Lieutenant Commander GS White, VC.

35. HMS E14.

36. Commander CC Dobson, VC.

37. Captain James McCudden, VC.

38. Major E Mannock, VC.

39. Squadron Leader RAM Palmer, VC.

40. A Handley Page Hampden bomber, as flown by Flight Lieutenant RAB Learoyd, VC.

41. Petty Officer TW Gould, VC.

42. Lieutenant Colonel AC Newman, VC.

43. Sergeant TF Durrant, VC.

44. Lieutenant GA Cairns, VC.

45. Lance Corporal JP Harman, VC.

46. Major WP Sidney, VC.

47. Captain LE Queripel, VC.

48. Captain JHC Brunt, VC.

49. Lance Corporal HE Harden, VC.

50. Lieutenant GA Knowlands, VC

In 1917 the regiment was involved in fierce fighting on the Hindenburg Line where it suffered appalling casualties; of the men who had arrived in France in 1914, only seventeen all ranks remained, including, it would seem, Christopher Bushell. At some point he was transferred to the 7th Battalion as temporary lieutenant colonel and it was whilst occupying this position that his actions resulted in him being awarded the Victoria Cross.

In late 1917 the German High Command decided that the following spring it would launch a decisive attack on the British army, which it believed to be exhausted by its four major efforts in 1917: Arras, Messines, Passchendaele and Cambrai. It is true that the British army was sorely depleted by these battles, was suffering a manpower crisis and needed to reorganize. Morale was at an all-time low and the men were not relishing the thought of having to fight a defensive battle for the first time since 1915.

Over the winter Germany moved many divisions from the now-collapsed Eastern Front to the Western, ultimately boasting 177 divisions, which gave it a significant numerical advantage. The German intention was to punch a hole in the British lines and then wheel north west to surround the British army and force it to surrender. The plan was an opportune one since the British 'line', which it had only just taken over from the French, barely existed in fact and much labour and construction was needed to put it into a defensible state. But there was no labour available and, when the battle opened, few of the defensive positions were ready and there were no reserve lines at all.

The German plan was to lay down an intensive and deep artillery barrage, designed to knock out the British ability to respond, followed quickly by infantry which would operate in small, infiltration groups to exploit any gaps, leaving the bypassed British positions to be mopped up by the next wave. The British, accustomed to having a continuous line, would have been disconcerted by such tactics, which would have led to chaos and disorder. It was a tactic that very nearly worked.

On 21 March 1918 the German offensive began as planned. The barrage wreaked enormous damage but the weary British and Allied troops were not prepared to give up now and fought back valiantly, repulsing the infantry attacks and even mounting counteroffensives. It was during one of the latter that Lieutenant Colonel Bushell personally led C Company of his battalion, which was cooperating with an Allied regiment, in a determined counterattack in the face of very heavy machine gun fire. He was severely wounded in the head but carried on, walking in front of both the British and the Allied troops, encouraging and reorganizing them. He rejected offers to dress his wound until he had got the whole line in a sound position and formed a defensive flank to meet any turning movement by the enemy. He then went to Brigade Headquarters, reported the situation and had his wound dressed before returning to the firing line, which had fallen back a short distance. He visited every portion of the line, both English and Allied, in the face of terrific machine gun and rifle fire, exhorting the troops to remain where they were and to kill the enemy. In spite of his painful and debilitating wound, he refused to go to the rear, and eventually had to be removed to the dressing station in a fainting condition.

It was this magnificent display of energy, courage and devotion to duty by their commanding officer that encouraged the battalion to put up a keen and spirited fight, not only on the day in question, but throughout the days of the withdrawal.

Lieutenant Colonel Bushell soon returned to duty and resumed command of the 7th Battalion. Early on the morning of 8 August 1918 he was leading his men in an attack on enemy positions south of Morlencourt when a situation arose. Accompanied by his runner, he gathered all available men and led them forward 'over the top' to engage the enemy, capturing one of its trenches. He then made his way along the trench to organize and encourage his men and was on his way to talk to a tank crew when a sniper got a bead on him and shot him in the head. His runner, ignoring the withering machine gun fire, rushed to his aid but when his body was recovered Lieutenant Colonel Bushell was found to be already dead.

Lieutenant Colonel Christopher Bushell, VC DSO was buried in the Querrieu British War Cemetery, France. His name appears on the St Margaret's-at-Cliffe war memorial and on a plaque inside Bishopsbourne Parish Church, near Canterbury, alongside that of his wife, Rachel Bushell MBE.

Upon Colonel Bushell's death, Rachel lived in Viscount Ipswich's former home at 114 Lower Bridge Street, Wye, before moving to Church Road, Boughton Aluph. In 1931 she continued the association with Kent by settling at Hooker's Green, Bishopsbourne, near Canterbury, where she became a churchwarden and was heavily involved in the Women's Voluntary Service, earning her an MBE in 1959. Although the last few years of her life, following the marriage of her daughter, were spent in the Canterbury

Cathedral precincts, when she died in 1965 her body was buried in Bishopsbourne churchyard, where a plaque celebrates the lives of both her and her husband, Lieutenant Colonel Christophe Bushell, VC DSO.

In 2004 the Ashford Borough Council approved the naming of a road in the town after Christopher Bushell, despite the fact that he had no real connections with the town. This caused something of an uproar since many residents of the town felt that there were other, more worthy candidates for the honour, such as Harry Wells, VC (see previous entry).

Captain Eric Stuart DOUGALL

The Royal Borough of Tunbridge Wells claims ten holders of the Victoria Cross, one of whom was Eric Stuart Dougall. Eric was born there on 13 April 1886, the son of Scotsman Andrew Dougall, who, like so many of his countrymen, was a chartered engineer. At the time of Eric's birth he was the general manager of the town's gas company and the family, which comprised Eric's mother, Emily Elizabeth Dougall, and his elder sister, Ellen, lived in the 'Gas House' at Brookside in Auckland Road, Tunbridge Wells.

Eric Dougall was educated at Tonbridge School and was awarded an exhibition to study engineering at Pembroke College, Cambridge where he won a Blue for athletics and was secretary of the university's Athletics Club. On graduating Eric was employed as an assistant engineer on the staff of the Bombay Port Trust, but when war broke out in 1914 he obtained leave of absence to return to England and, in January 1916, volunteered as a gunner in the Royal Horse Artillery. He was gazetted as a second lieutenant in the Royal Field Artillery the following July and saw service on the Somme with the BEF. Promoted lieutenant in January 1917, he took part in the various battles in the Ypres sector.

In May 1917 he was made acting captain and the following month took part in the Battle of Messines when the British Second Army launched an offensive near the village of Messines (Mesen) in West Flanders, Belgium. One of the key features of this battle was the detonation of nineteen mines immediately prior to the infantry assault, which disrupted the German defences and enabled the advancing troops to secure their objectives very quickly. It was during this action that Eric Dougall was awarded the Military Cross for 'for gallantry in the field'.

On 4 April 1918 Lieutenant (acting captain) Dougall was promoted to acting major and only ten days later was present when, at dawn on 9 April

1918, in thick fog, the Germans launched a major offensive on the Lys sector between Béthune and Ypres. Heavy fighting continued throughout the day, only lessening as night fell, by which time the Germans had created a large breach.

The German attack was renewed early the next day, extending north to the Messines Ridge, preceded by a concentrated gas and high-explosive artillery bombardment. At this time Captain Dougall was commanding an artillery battery covering the ridge. As the British line withdrew he found he was unable to clear the crest and so ran his guns on to the top of the ridge in order to fire over open sights. By this time the British infantry had been pressed back to positions in line with the guns and, observing the chaos and disorder, Captain Dougall took command of the situation. He rallied and organized the infantry, supplied them with Lewis guns and armed as many of his Royal Artillery gunners as he could spare with any available rifles, using them to form a line in front of his battery of guns. Meantime, the guns were harassing the enemy with a rapid rate of fire.

Although exposed to both rifle and machine gun fire Captain Dougall walked fearlessly about the men as though on parade, calmly giving orders and encouraging them all. He inspired the infantry by assuring them that 'So long as you stick to your trenches I will keep my guns here.' Thus encouraged, the line held throughout the day, thereby holding up the enemy's advance for more than twelve hours. By the evening all his ammunition had been exhausted and the battery was given orders to withdraw. The only way to accomplish this was by manhandling the guns over about 800 yards of shell-cratered terrain – an almost-impossible feat, considering the ground and the intense machine gun fire. There is no doubt that Captain Dougall's personality and skilful leadership throughout a very trying day averted a serious breach in the British line. The award of the Victoria Cross to him was well deserved.

Sadly, this brave Kentish man was killed four days later whilst directing the fire of his battery on Mount Kemmel. His body is buried in the British Military Cemetery, Westoutre.

His adjutant wrote of him: 'A finer man never lived and his place in the Brigade can never be filled ... He was in command of his battery at the time of his death and for the past week had been performing most gallant work.'

These complimentary comments were echoed by the chaplain: 'Seldom have I met an officer who commanded such unbounded devotion from his men and unqualified admiration from his fellow officers, and I always considered that in him was found the most perfect example of a "man" in the highest form of the word.'

Sergeant Thomas HARRIS

Thomas Harris was the son of William John and Sarah Ann Harris of Halling, Kent, the seventh child in a family of nine children. This was not a rich family. William was a labourer in the cement industry – the dominant employer in that area – and his large family must have known considerable hardships. Thomas was born on 30 January 1892 and after leaving Halling Board School went to work at the Manor Cement Works.

When the Great War began Thomas Harris was twenty-two and he immediately enlisted, joining the newly formed 6th (Service) Battalion of the Queen's Own Royal West Kent Regiment on 27 August 1914. The battalion was initially posted to Colchester but then moved on in turn to Purfleet, Hythe and Aldershot, before travelling to Boulogne on 1 June 1915. Thomas was made a lance corporal in July 1915 and promoted to corporal on 1 June 1916.

During 1916 he was wounded on two occasions. Following the first occasion, on 26 February 1916, he was treated in a field hospital and returned to duty on 12 March 1916. On 2 July 1916 he received a further wound to his right side that entailed his return to England and his confinement in hospital until 25 August 1916. He did not return to France and to the trenches until 23 May 1917.

On 21 March 1918, following a 5-hour bombardment by over 6,000 guns, 1,000,000 German soldiers attacked along a 50-mile front opposite the British Third and Fifth armies. The Fifth Army fell back towards Amiens in the face of the onslaught and the 10th Battalion of the Royal West Kents suffered badly during the first few days. The 6th Battalion, in which Corporal Harris was serving, was hastily brought in from Pont de Nieppe to take over the task of trying to stem the German advance, arriving at the front early on 25 March after a long and tiring journey by bus.

After some hours of waiting, orders were issued for the battalion to take up an outpost line near Ovillers, where on 27 March a serious attack on the 6th Royal West Kents was repulsed, but that evening at around 6pm the Germans renewed their attack. They had already forced back the troops further to the left and so the Royal West Kents had to withdraw to ensure the continuity of the line. The pressure on the battalion was severe: one attack along the whole line was beaten off, but a little later the enemy drove B Company back to the railway line, where it made a stand. The next morning saw the battalion subjected to an intense bombardment and the enemy succeeded in making its position untenable, causing B Company to fall back once more until a counter attack dislodged the enemy.

The Royal West Kents won a number of medals in this engagement and, promoted to acting sergeant on 28 March 1918, Thomas Harris was awarded the Military Medal for his part in the fighting during the period 25–28 March 1918. His promotion to sergeant was confirmed on 24 June 1918.

In August 1918 the 1st, 6th and 7th Battalions of the Royal West Kent Regiment played a prominent role in the first phase of General Haig's Amiens offensive. On 8 August, the 7th Battalion was actively engaged in an attack, while the 6th Battalion was held in reserve and spent the day in readiness. That evening it moved up, ready to continue the attack next morning.

After several postponements, the attack was renewed at 5.30pm, assisted by tanks and under a creeping barrage. The advance of the 6th Royal West Kents was met with considerable opposition from machine guns skillfully concealed in the cornfields and in shell holes, and for a time the attack seemed bound to be held up. That this did not happen was due to the gallantry and devotion of Sergeant Harris, who rushed one of these guns at the head of his section and captured it, killing seven of the enemy. Twice more as the advance proceeded the same thing happened, each time Sergeant Harris dashed forward against the obstructing machine gun. In the first instance he was again successful, killing the whole team single-handedly; the second time he was himself shot dead, but his example had inspired all those round him and the advance swept on.

Thomas Harris was posthumously awarded the Victoria Cross for his actions during this attack. An extract from the *London Gazette* dated 22 October 1918 records the following:

For most conspicuous bravery and devotion to duty in attack, His Majesty the King has been graciously pleased to approve the award of the Victoria Cross to No. G/358 Sjt. Thomas James Harris, MM, late Royal West Kent Regiment (Lower Halling, Kent). It was largely due the great courage and initiative of this gallant N.C.O. that the advance of the battalion was continued without delay and undue casualties. Throughout the operation he showed a total disregard for his own personal safety, and set a magnificent example to all ranks.

Thomas's platoon commander, Second Lieutenant SJ Upfold, who was with him on the final attempt and was wounded in the attack but survived, later wrote to Thomas's parents of the events of that evening:

September 27th, 1918.

Dear Mrs. Harris,

It is with a feeling of profound sympathy that I address myself to you. The blow you have sustained in the loss of your extremely gallant son is an irreparable one, and I feel very deeply with you and your husband in your bereavement. I was the officer in charge of the platoon to which your son was attached, and was the only person near him when he was killed, for as a matter of fact we were within a yard of one another when the bullets struck him and he fell into my arms. His death was practically instantaneous, for he just smiled, sent his love to his mother and his father, wished me good-bye, and his gallant spirit was gone to the place where there is no pain, and where suffering is unknown. He was killed by fire from a machine gun which was holding up the whole advance, and at the time he was assisting me in an endeavour to get at it and silence it. This was on the evening of the 9th August, and we were about half-way through an attack … We had gone over about 6.30 p.m., and went forward in the face of very heavy machine gun fire. Sergeant Harris performed many heroic acts, and behaved with the utmost gallantry, not once, but continually, and his example was a very fine one to the men. I have never seen a braver man, totally unafraid, doing his duty nobly, with an utter disregard for his own personal safety, and encouraging his men splendidly. He covered himself with glory, and I afterwards put his name forward as worthy of decoration. His valour was remarkable, and he was a credit to himself, to his Regiment, and to his parents. Earlier in the attack, while the whole Company was held up by machine gun fire, he went forward alone, without waiting for orders, and rushed the gun, killing some of the crew, and compelling the remainder to surrender. He met his death while accompanying me in getting another gun. I had crawled forward towards it, and in gathering myself together for a final rush, discovered that your son, with a devotion that touched me very, very deeply, had crawled after me, refusing to allow me to go forward without assistance, and, unasked, had taken it upon himself to share the risk with me. It was the most magnificent thing one man could do for another and it is only on such occasions, when death is all round, that one discovers the worth of a man like your son. The moment we got up Sergeant Harris dashed forward and was shot down by my side. With his last breath came the message for his mother, indeed his last thoughts were for you, and if anything can be a satisfaction to you under the weight of such a blow, I personally saw to it that not one of the machine gun crew were left alive, for I was as upset as though he had been my own brother, for he was such an extremely devoted NCO, that I had grown to develop a great respect for his courage and ability. I did all I could for him, but it was impossible to save his life, because he was killed almost at once and suffered no pain. He was buried afterwards close to Dernancourt. Personally I experienced a feeling of great loss when he went, for I had a good deal to do with him, and many opportunities of judging his sterling worth. I always found him absolutely trustworthy, full of the most sublime courage, and always willing to do more than his duty under any circumstances. All the officers thought very highly of him, and he was exceedingly popular with the men. Magnificent under fire he performed prodigies of valour and was absolutely invaluable to me. He died very gallantly, faithful to the last, and I reported his exceptional bravery to the higher authorities after we had ultimately reached our objective. I wish to tender you my very deepest and most heartfelt sympathy and to assure you that you have every reason to be proud of so gallant a son as Sergeant Harris.

SJ UPFOLD, 2nd Lieut., RWKR

Thomas' mother, Sarah, replied to Lieutenant Upfold immediately but no details of her letter are available. His response in October, when he expressed further sympathy to the family and spoke of his slow recovery, was as follows:

11th October, 1918.

Dear Mrs. Harris,

Thank you for your letter and for your kindly expressed sympathy with me. I am very glad to have been able to have told you all you wanted to know about your extremely gallant son, and you may indeed feel justly proud of him. Germany can never hope to win when such men as your son are in the British Army. It is, of course, a very heavy blow to lose him, but it softens the pain when you know he met his end as a real hero, a credit to you, to himself, and to his Regiment. I can sympathise with you very deeply, for I lost my favourite brother out there, and I know the awful agony such a thing means; but, believe me, a man is not afraid to die when, by risking his life he is keeping those loved ones at home from the awful horrors we have had proof that invasion by the unspeakable Hun means. Your son died for England and for the cause of Right, but he died too, that all whom he loved might live, and it is the greatest thing a man can do. I am glad to say that I am getting along pretty well, although they tell me that it will take a long time for me to get right.

SJ UPFOLD, 2nd Lieut., RWKR.

One day later he wrote again with the news that Thomas Harris had been awarded the Victoria Cross:

12th October, 1918.

Dear Mrs. Harris,

I am extremely glad to be able to inform you that I have just received a letter from my Colonel in France, telling me that your son, Sergeant Harris has won undying fame, for His Majesty the King has been pleased to bestow upon him the highest honour a soldier can ever hope to attain, i.e., the Victoria Cross. The Colonel will be personally writing to you. In your great sorrow, the great honour won by your son will bring you consolation, for it will show more clearly than words of mine can express how magnificently he behaved, and I can assure you that I am proud to have been with him, proud to have shared his exploits, proud, immensely proud, to have been his officer. Not only has he won fame for himself and honour to his family, but he has also brought it to the Regiment he loved so well, for he is the first V.C. of the Royal West Kent Regiment. I know nothing can lessen the pain caused by his loss, but you have now the glorious knowledge that he was the bravest and most gallant man in the Regiment, and you have every reason to be proud of him who has brought such great honour to you. Sympathising with you as I do, I am happy to be the first to notify you of this, and to offer you my very heartiest congratulations, for although your gallant son has fallen, his name will live for ever, to be emblazoned on the scroll of fame as one of England's heroes.

SJ UPFOLD, MC, 2nd Lieut., R. West Kent Rgt.

P.S. I have been awarded the Military Cross.

The *Rochester, Chatham and Gillingham News* of 19 October 1918 had this to say:

A Halling Hero. Posthumous Award of the Victoria Cross.

Mr. and Mrs. W Harris, of 6 Manor Terrace, Halling, have this week received the gratifying news that the VC has been posthumously awarded to their gallant son, Sergeant Thomas James Harris, Royal West Kent Regiment, aged 24 [sic] years (whose death was announced in *The News* of September 14th), for conspicuous bravery on the battlefield. We append copies of letters that have been received by his mother from the Officer Commanding his platoon, that speak volumes for the valour of the deceased sergeant. Although the 'Fighting West Kents' have performed many heroic deeds, and covered themselves with glory in the present great war, it is a fact that no individual soldier or officer had been previously awarded the much-coveted VC. The decoration will therefore be doubly prized by his bereaved parents. Sergeant Harris received his education in the Halling Council School, consequently the Headmaster, staff, pupils and managers rejoice at the honour done to his memory, and a similar feeling prevails among his late employers and fellow workmen, and among the residents generally.

The medal itself was presented to Thomas's parents after the war by the King in a ceremony at Buckingham Palace and later it passed to their son, Herbert George. Some years later the family donated both medals, the VC and MM, to the Queen's Own Royal West Kent Regiment, and today they are on display in its museum at Maidstone.

Lieutenant Cecil Harold SEWELL

Cecil Sewell came from a long-standing Kentish family. His grandfather, George Robbins Sewell, was a carpenter, born and bred in Ramsgate, where he lived until 1861 and where Cecil's father, Harry Bolton Sewell, was born in 1859, although the family moved to Rotherhithe when Harry was just two years old. Further moves meant that Harry spent most of his life in Greenwich, which was then very much part of Kent.

Some sources suggest that on leaving school Harry Sewell worked as a railway clerk but what is certain is that by 1901 the forty-two-year-old Kentish man had qualified as a solicitor and had his own practice with a staff of helpers. He was then living at 26 Crooms Hill, Greenwich with his wife, Mary Ann Kemp, whom he had married in 1882, and their extensive family of five sons and four daughters. Unusually for such a large, well-to-do family in those days, there is no record of any live-in servants, but perhaps the family employed local staff to attend to the domestic chores on a live-out basis. Certainly, with nine children, ranging in age from three to eighteen, there would have been little room in the house for staff.

In 1914 the thirty-year-old eldest son, Harry (junior), was a deputy coroner for Kent while Herbert (twenty-four) was a barrister. Cecil, the youngest at nineteen (born 27 January 1895), was now also studying law. But when war broke out that August they and their two other brothers, Frank and Leonard, together with their father, all volunteered for military service. Henry Bolton Sewell, by now fifty-five years of age, joined the Royal Army Medical Corps and served in the Balkans and Mesopotamia. Frank Sewell, the second-eldest son, served as a lieutenant in the Royal Garrison Artillery while brother Leonard was a corporal in the Honourable Artillery Company. These two sons, together with their father, both survived the war but Harry junior, Herbert and Cecil all died, the latter earning the Victoria Cross.

Cecil Harold Sewell, the youngest son of the family, had been educated at Dulwich College between 1907 and 1910 and matriculated at London University. In 1912 he was articled to his father with a view to qualifying as a solicitor and in 1914 joined the Public Schools Battalion, 21st Royal Fusiliers (Machine Gun Section) as a private soldier. After service in France in this capacity, he was sent home and passed through a Cadet Battalion, gaining a commission in the 3rd Battalion, the Queen's Own Royal West Kent Regiment in August 1916. He returned to France and shortly afterwards transferred to the heavy branch of the Machine Gun Corps (the precursor to the Tank Corps) and saw considerable service with heavy tanks.

In the closing stages of the war he was attached to the newly formed 3rd (Light) Battalion of the Tank Corps. This battalion had been equipped with the new Whippet light tank at the end of 1917 and these first went into action in March 1918, providing invaluable cover for the infantry divisions recoiling from the German onslaught during the Spring Offensive. In one incident a single Whippet company of seven tanks wiped out two entire battalions of German infantry caught in the open, killing over 400.

In August 1918 the 3rd Battalion's forty-eight Whippets were involved in the Amiens offensive, described by the German supreme commander, General Ludendorff, as the 'Black Day of the German Army'. The Whippets broke through into the German rear areas, causing havoc to the enemy's artillery. One tank advanced so far that it was cut off behind enemy lines and for nine hours it roamed as it pleased, destroying artillery and infantry alike, causing great damage and casualties.

During this offensive, on 29 August 1918, Lieutenant Cecil Sewell was in command of a section of Whippet tanks at Frémicourt, near Bapaume, when one of them side-slipped into a shell crater, overturned and caught fire. The door of the tank was jammed up against the side of the shell hole and the crew were unable to escape. With the tank 'brewing-up', it seemed certain that they would all perish in the flames.

However, Lieutenant Sewell, grasping the situation, leapt out of his own tank and, crossing an expanse of open ground exposed to heavy shell, machine gun and rifle fire, somehow managed to gain the relative safety of the shell hole without being hit. Unaided, he then dug away at the loose earth, blocking the tank's hatch and enabled the three men inside to escape what would have been a certain and very unpleasant death. Looking back towards his own tank, Lieutenant Sewell saw that one of his crew was lying wounded behind the tank, and so he re-crossed the exposed terrain to get to him. In doing so he was hit but managed to gain the shelter of the tank and began to tend to his crewman's wound. It was whilst so doing that he was hit again, this time fatally. During the whole of this period he was in full view and close range of the enemy machine guns and rifle pits and showed an utter disregard for his own personal safety. The award of the Victoria Cross was published in the *London Gazette* on 29 October 1918.

Cecil's mother, Mary Ann, died in Greenwich in 1928 at the age of sixty-nine but her husband, Henry Bolton Sewell, survived for a further thirteen years, dying peacefully at his retirement home in Worthing in 1941 at the age of eighty-two.

The Victoria Cross, which was presented to Cecil Sewell's proud parents by King George V at Buckingham Palace on 13 December 1918 (following the Armistice), is now held at the Royal Tank Regiment Museum, Bovington, Dorset, together with his Whippet tank. Lieutenant Cecil Harold Sewell lies buried at the Vaulx Hill Cemetery, Vaulx-Vraucourt, France, unlike his brother, Harry, whose body was never found following his death on the Somme in 1916.

Lieutenant Donald DEAN

The name Dean was, and still is, a well-known one in the Sittingbourne area. George Hambrook Dean was born in the town around 1835 and followed his father into the tailoring and drapery business, occupying premises in the High Street. By the time George was twenty-six, however, he was a farmer employing six men and a boy at Finches in Milstead, was married to Mary and had three daughters. Over the years the couple added two sons, the younger being John Hambrook Dean, born in 1866, the father of the subject of this item, Donald John Dean, VC. The family were now living at Whitehall, Bell Road, Sittingbourne, in what was to become the family seat.

By 1880, George Hambrook Dean was widowed and had abandoned farming for a while to become the partner of George Smeed, a well-known and prosperous brick manufacturer. George Smeed died in 1881 but the firm of Smeed Dean & Co continues to make bricks to this day. In due course George Dean remarried and was described as a land owner and justice of the peace for the county. As the world moved into the twentieth century, the sixty-five-year-old George Hambrook Dean was still living at Whitehall with his second wife Jane (who had herself become a justice of the peace) and was now described as a farmer, jam maker and brick manufacturer – a somewhat curious mixture of occupations!

John Hambrook Dean, George's second son, was educated at Christ's Hospital School in London and, on leaving, went into the family firm as the London representative of Smeed Dean & Co, no doubt selling the firm's famous London Yellow Stock bricks, which were being produced by the millions on the site of the old Murston manor. John married Grace Walduck in 1891 and they moved to Herne Hill, Surrey, where the couple soon had three sons, Graham, Donald and Harold. The family then took up residence in Lambeth no doubt to be nearer John's work but, by the time the First World War began the family were back in Kent, living at Waldene in Tunstall.

Donald John Dean was born on 19 April 1897 and was therefore only just seventeen when the war started. He did not allow this to deter him, however: lying about his age, he volunteered in the autumn of 1914 for the 28th London (Artists' Rifles) Regiment, with which he served, as a private soldier, in the Ypres Salient and during the Battle of the Somme. He was commissioned as a second lieutenant in October 1916 and joined the 11th Battalion of the Royal West Kent Regiment, seeing action at Vimy Ridge and around Givenchy. In 1918 the 11th Battalion was disbanded and he became a temporary lieutenant with the 8th (S) Battalion of the same regiment.

On 24 September 1918, he and half of his platoon from D Company were holding an advance post in a newly captured German position, known as Canary Trench, somewhere to the north west of Lens. This position had changed hands several times in the past and the enemy made repeated attempts to regain it over the next two days, but were continually repulsed by Lieutenant Dean's party. During every lull between onslaughts and throughout the night, the young officer set his men to work repairing and improving the fortifications, ready for the next attack.

About 6am on 25 September 1918 a heavy barrage was put down that completely isolated the post but the defenders never wavered and continued to fight off the ensuing infantry assault. Once this early morning excitement had died down the day passed relatively quietly and the second half of the platoon arrived to relieve their comrades. However, Lieutenant Dean insisted on remaining in charge with the new arrivals. The next day saw an early but half-hearted attack by the Germans, which was easily fought off, but this was followed by an intense bombardment that forced the remnants of the garrison back around fifty yards, enabling the jubilant Germans to rush and take the temporarily abandoned position. Their triumph was not to last long. Lieutenant Dean rallied his shaken troops and, aided by men from a neighbouring position, launched a counter attack across the open and exposed terrain. The startled German troops suffered heavy casualties and quickly bolted, leaving the British to re-occupy the trench. It was for his 'most conspicuous bravery, skilful command and devotion to duty' during the two days of this action that Lieutenant Donald Dean was awarded the Victoria Cross. His platoon sergeant, Sergeant Skinner, was given the Distinguished Conduct Medal while four others received the Military Medal. In all, this little band of infantrymen had fought off five attacks, three of them by greatly superior numbers. Lieutenant Dean personally shot four Germans and on one occasion was speaking to his company commander on the field telephone, saying, 'They are shelling us rather badly. Can we get some retaliation? The shells seem to be coming from all directions.' Then he suddenly broke off, saying, 'The Germans are here. Goodbye.'

Lieutenant Donald Dean did not escape unscathed from the war. He was wounded four times, twice on the same day, but happily survived to live a long life. He continued to serve in the army, transferring to the 4th Battalion of the Buffs at Dibgate Camp, Shorncliffe, in 1921. When the Second World War broke out in 1939, Major Dean was placed in charge of No 5 Group Auxiliary Pioneer Corps in France. The group was heavily engaged in the defence of Boulogne (during which Donald Dean was blown up and mistakenly reported as killed in action) and then covered the withdrawal of the Guards off the beaches at Dunkirk. The group was among the last to leave the beaches at Dunkirk and Dean was promoted lieutenant colonel on his return to England. He later served in Madagascar, where he was responsible for organizing the return of the defeated Vichy forces to France. Colonel Dean took part in the Sicily landings in 1943 and later served in Italy. He was twice mentioned in despatches and retired after the war with the rank of full colonel and an OBE.

Colonel Donald Dean inherited his parents' home at Waldene, Tunstall, and it was here that he died on 9 December 1985 at the age of eighty-eight. His ashes were buried in the churchyard of St John the Baptist Church, Tunstall, and the inscription on his headstone reads: 'I have fought a good fight, I have finished my course, I have kept the faith.' He was the last surviving holder of the Victoria Cross from the First World War.

The War at Sea

Understandably, references to the First World War usually conjure up images of the troops fighting in the trenches in France and Flanders but, of course, the war was also fought at sea. Britain has always been a seafaring nation and its navy is referred to as the Senior Service. The battles at sea were much fewer than those on land but the loss of life was also high and the bravery of the British seamen equal to their landlubber comrades.

Lieutenant Ronald Neil STUART, RNR

During the First World War, the German Imperial Navy attempted to blockade Britain and so force it to capitulate, using its fleet of U boats to cut off food and vital supplies. Its main targets were the unarmed merchant vessels that were easy prey to these marauding submarines. To combat this threat the Royal Navy began using armed vessels, disguised as ordinary cargo ships, and known as 'Q' ships or 'mystery' ships. Deliberately inviting attack, the aim of the Q ships was to entice the U boat to surface in order to destroy the apparently unarmed vessel and, once it did so, it would reveal its formidable weaponry and hopefully sink the surfaced submarine instead. It was whilst serving on such a vessel, HMS *Pargust*, that Ronald Stuart earned his Victoria Cross.

Ronald Stuart was born on 26 August 1886 in Toxteth Park, Liverpool, the son of Neil Stuart, a Canadian master mariner of Scottish descent. His father and his mother, Mary, spent most of their time on the high seas between England and Australia. It is even said that Ronald (the youngest of a family of six) was conceived on one of these trips! Neil and Mary were married in Montreal but moved south, where Neil became a river boat skipper on the Mississippi, later returning to England and settling in Liverpool.

Educated at Shaw Street College, Liverpool, Ronald Neil Stuart's education came to an abrupt end with the death of his father in an accident. A brief spell in an office soon convinced Ronald that this was not the life for him and so he went to sea when he was just sixteen, his first vessel as an apprentice being the sailing barque *Kirkhill*, which foundered, with Ronald on board, off the Falkland Islands in 1905. Over the next decade Ronald increased his seamanship and maritime qualifications and ultimately worked for the Canadian Pacific Line. When the First World War began in 1914 he was a junior officer on one of the Canadian Pacific's large steamships but, in 1916, he was commissioned into the Royal Naval Reserve (RNR) and served on various Royal Navy ships, earning him the Distinguished Service Order. In 1916 he was a lieutenant and selected to join the crew of the Q ship HMS *Pargust* under Commander Gordon Campbell, who was himself to win the VC in February 1917 whilst commanding another Q ship.

On 7 June 1917 HMS *Pargust* was on the Atlantic Ocean when it was hit by a torpedo, fired at very close range by a German submarine. Her boiler room, engine room and hold were immediately flooded and the starboard lifeboat was blown to pieces. The weather was misty at the time, with a light breeze and choppy seas. In accordance with prearranged plans, a 'panic party' – complete with a stuffed parrot in a cage – took to the remaining lifeboats to make the enemy believe that the vessel was being abandoned and, as the last lifeboat was pulling away, the U boat's periscope was spotted some 400 yards away. The submarine circled the stricken vessel and eventually surfaced about fifty yards away.

Acting as a lure, the lifeboat began to pull away round the stern and the submarine duly followed until it was fully exposed to HMS *Pargust*'s disguised armament, which then opened up with all guns. Despite the fact that she was sinking, the Q boat continued firing until the enemy boat sank. Only two German seamen were recovered and the damaged ship was taken on tow by a sloop and brought back to Queenstown.

To deliberately offer oneself as a target demands great courage on the part of all the crew and so, in accordance with Rule 13 of the Royal Warrant, the Victoria Cross was awarded by ballot to one officer and one rating to represent the crew as a whole. The officers' ballot resulted in Lieutenant Ronald Stuart, who had been in command of the gun party, being chosen for this honour, while the ratings chose one of their number, Welshman William Williams, who already held the Distinguished Service Medal, to receive theirs.

Promoted to lieutenant commander, Ronald Stuart went on to command his own Q ships and in October 1917 he went to the assistance of the American destroyer USS *Cassin* when it was torpedoed by a U boat. The destroyer's stern was blown off, rendering her uncontrollable, and Lieutenant Commander Stuart, who was then commanding the Q ship *Tamarisk*, with great difficulty and at great risk of losing his own vessel, got a line to the *Cassin* and succeeded in towing her to port. For his heroic actions he was awarded the United States' Navy Cross, although this was not announced until ten years later.

After the war Ronald Stuart returned to the Canadian Pacific Line but continued to be in the RNR, being promoted to commander in 1928 and captain in 1935. In civilian life, he commanded several of the Canadian Pacific Railway's ships, eventually being appointed commander of the SS *Empress of Britain* and commodore of the Canadian Pacific Line fleet. He ultimately became the London manager of the CPR, retiring in 1951. In 1941 he was the Naval Aide-de-Camp to King George VI.

His wife, Evelyn Wright, whom he married in 1919, died in 1931 and he was left to raise his three sons and two daughters on his own. His four surviving sisters, none of whom married, helped him in this and for the rest of his life he lived with them at Beryl Lodge in Charing, Kent, where he died in 1954 at the age of sixty-seven.

Ronald Stuart was described as a complex, sometimes irascible man who abhorred pomp and snobbery. He rarely spoke of his war experiences and was said to be embarrassed by any fuss surrounding his notoriety or any displays of emotion. He never took a holiday or indulged in any kind of social life outside his work and was greatly affected by his wife's death. Although he was only in his mid-forties at the time, he never remarried. Two of his sons followed naval careers, one in the Royal Navy and the other in the Royal Canadian Navy, the former gaining the DSO in the Second World War.

Captain Ronald Neil Stuart, VC DSO RD RNR was buried in the local parish cemetery in Charing. His medals, including the Victoria Cross, are held by the National Maritime Museum in London.

Lieutenant Commander Geoffrey Saxton WHITE

While the Q ships described earlier were used to seek and destroy enemy U boats during the First World War, another branch of the Royal Navy was itself using submarines. It might be said that every man aboard these vessels was a hero, but none more so than the young Lieutenant Commander Geoffrey White.

Geoffrey Saxton White was born in Bromley on 2 July 1886 but when he was still a toddler the family, consisting of father, William Henry White, mother, Alice White, elder brother, Frank Saxton White, and young Geoffrey, moved to Reigate, where they lived in some considerable comfort in Charlwood Park House. This small family in fact employed no fewer than ten servants! William Henry White was described as living on private means but it is not known whether these were inherited or amassed by his own efforts. In 1881, at the age of thirty-four, William was living in Croydon and was recorded as being a clerk in a Bounty Office. Whether this is where he made his fortune is not known but, since his father (Geoffrey Saxon's grandfather) seems to have been a bricklayer in Camberwell, this was certainly a meteoric rise in the family fortunes.

As young Geoffrey Saxon White began to grow up he was packed off to Bradfield College in Reading, leaving at the age of sixteen to enter the Royal Navy as a midshipman. He served on a number of capital ships before being assigned to the nascent submarine branch in 1909. He commanded various submarines from 1911 to early 1914 when he was assigned to the battleship HMS *Monarch*. In Navy parlance, he returned to 'the Trade' in September 1916 and took command of the submarine E14 in 1916 – coincidentally the same submarine as previously commanded by Lieutenant Commander Edward Boyle, who won the VC in the Dardanelles in 1915.

By 1918, the abortive Gallipoli campaign was long over, but there was still considerable naval activity off the Turkish coast, intended primarily to prevent the German battle cruiser SMS *Goeben* and the light cruiser SMS *Breslau* breaking out, they having been handed over to the Turks in 1914. This containment proved effective until January 1918 when these two vessels slipped out of the Dardanelles, with the intention of attacking the British base at Mudros. Their project foundered, however, when the *Breslau* struck several mines and rapidly sank. The *Goeben* also struck two mines but remained afloat, albeit at the mercy of attacks by British aircraft, and began to limp back towards Constantinople (now Istanbul). When she was about fifteen miles from the mouth of the Dardanelles she ran helplessly aground off Nagara Point. Sustained aerial attacks failed to inflict much damage on this heavily armoured warship and so Lieutenant Commander Geoffrey White was instructed to proceed in the E14 to finish the job.

The E14 sailed from Mudros on 27 January 1918 under orders to force the Narrows (where the Dardanelles Strait is only 1,600 metres wide) and attack the *Goeben* where she lay stranded. During the night the E14 had to find its way through an extensive system of anti-submarine nets and in the early hours of the next morning, at the entrance to the Narrows, fouled a net, which forced it on to a sandbank in about 19 feet of water. Unable to clear this obstruction, the vessel surfaced and Geoffrey White himself went out on deck to clear it, having instructed his first lieutenant, Mr Blissett, to dive at once if he called out, in order to save the ship's complement of two officers and thirty men. As it happens, the E14 was undetected and was able to continue unmolested.

Having reached Nagara Point the submarine was unable to locate its target. In fact, the *Goeben* had been refloated only a few hours before the E14 got there and so the submarine turned back to return to base. Around 8.45am that morning, 28 January, the E14 fired a torpedo at an enemy ship and eleven seconds later a heavy explosion occurred, causing all the lights to go out on the submarine and springing the fore hatch. It later transpired that the targeted enemy vessel was carrying ammunition from the *Goeben*, hence the violence of the explosion. Leaking badly, the submarine was blown to a depth of 15 feet and immediately came under heavy fire from the forts, but the hull was not damaged so she dived to 190 feet and proceeded on her way out.

Soon afterwards, sailing at 21 feet, the boat became unsteady and uncontrollable, heeling heavily to starboard and diving by the nose. As the air was nearly exhausted, Lieutenant Commander White decided to surface and run the gauntlet of fire from the shore-based batteries on either side of the straits, which commenced as soon as they broke surface. After half an hour the crippled submarine was so badly damaged it was incapable of diving, so Lieutenant Commander White had no option but to head for the shore in order to give the crew a chance of rescue. He remained on deck, declaring 'We are in the hands of God,' and a few seconds later he was almost blown to pieces by a shell. His remains were never recovered.

All the officers and many crew men were killed or drowned and the few survivors who made it to the shore were taken prisoner. One survivor was the coxswain, Petty Officer RA Perkins, on whose official report much of the above detail is based. The E14 sank in deep water, undoubtedly taking a number of the crew with her on her final dive.

Commander Claude Congreve Dobson

Claude Congreve Dobson was born in Barton Regis (formerly Clifton), Somerset on New Year's Day 1885, the son of Nelson Congreve Dobson, a surgeon and Fellow of the Royal College of Surgeons, and his wife, Louisa Alice Pierce. Nelson's father, Claude's grandfather, had been a veterinary surgeon in Lincolnshire but Claude was not destined for a medical career. Between the ages of eight and fifteen he attended Clifton College public school before becoming a naval cadet on the *Britannia* in Dartmouth in

1899. He progressed through the ranks of the Royal Navy and served in submarines during the First World War.

On 20 July 1915 Claude Dobson was in command of submarine C-27 which was being towed by a trawler when a German U boat, U23, surfaced in order to shell the trawler, causing the trawler's crew to cast off the tow and abandon ship. However, Dobson was able to fire two torpedoes, the second of which sank the U boat. This was in fact one of the earliest occasions on which trawlers had been used as decoys (like the 'Q' or 'mystery' ships) in order to prompt enemy submarines to surface and so be destroyed. For his actions in this incident, Dobson was awarded the Distinguished Service Order.

Later in the war, in the manner of poacher turned gamekeeper, Claude Dobson joined the Admiralty's Anti-Submarine Division and, subsequently, the newly formed Coastal Motor Boat service. It was in this latter role that Dobson became involved in the Russian conflict.

By 1919 the Armistice had been signed and the Great War was now over, but there still remained a few trouble spots involving military action. In Russia, the Bolsheviks had overthrown the Tsar, assassinating the whole of the Russian Royal family, and conflict continued in a civil war between the so-called White (Tsarist) and Red (Bolshevik) Russians. With the British Royal Family's close ties with their Russian relatives it was not surprising that Great Britain was throwing its weight behind the White Russian elements and was officially at war with the revolutionary regime and providing supplies to the supporters of the monarchy. A great many of these supplies had been stockpiled in Kronstadt, Murmansk, Archangel and other Russian ports and the problem arose as to how these could be protected from the Red Army. Kronstadt was a particular problem since the port – the key to Petrograd (St Petersburg) – had fallen into Bolshevik hands. The port was protected by a number of heavily armed forts, forming a chain between the island where the Russian harbour was situated and the mainland. There were also extensive minefields and underwater breakwaters, which presented a serious hazard to any shipping other than craft with a very shallow draught. However, a previous daring raid by two Coastal Motor Boats had been successful and so it was in the light of these circumstances that Commander Claude Dobson was instructed to lead a flotilla of motor boats in an action to cripple the enemy ships in the harbour and so safeguard the supplies.

Eight Coastal Motor Boats were towed out of their base near Clacton but one sank en route. The tow-lines of the others frequently broke but the remaining seven boats reached the port of Biorko in Finland. Having made a number of flights over the area to determine where the enemy vessels were, Commander Dobson decided that, in addition to the main target of two Russian battleships, there was a depot ship there which should also be targeted to deny supplies to the troublesome Russian submarines. There were also at least three cruisers in the harbour and a destroyer guarding the approach.

On the night of 17/18 August 1919, Commander Claude Dobson led eight high-speed Coastal Motor Boats from their base in Finland towards Kronstadt harbour. Each boat had a crew of three: a commanding officer at the wheel, a second officer to fire the torpedoes and a mechanic to look after the engines. They also carried a local guide to act as pilot should the need arise.

The boats formed up outside the harbour in two groups, the first being led by Lieutenant Bremner, whose boat was equipped to deal with any boom they might encounter. There were no booms so Bremner went straight in and torpedoed the supply ship, which sank almost immediately. Commander Dobson was next on CMB 31 and he successfully torpedoed the battle cruiser *Petropavlosk* while a third boat, despite its captain being mortally wounded, torpedoed the battleship, *Andrei Pervozvanni*.

The resulting noise alerted the shore garrisons, which had been sheltering from a diversionary air raid by the RAF, and all hell broke loose. Wending their way through the chain of forts protecting the harbour, the little boats were subjected to heavy machine gun and naval gun fire and the motor boat detailed to sink the guard destroyer was itself sunk by its intended target. Two boats collided in the harbour entrance, the least damaged picking up the crew of the other before it was itself hit by the Russian destroyer.

The remaining four boats managed to reach the open sea despite heavy opposition. Between them, the little motor boats had sunk a submarine depot ship, a battleship and a battle cruiser. The British raiders lost three of the CMBs and a number of officers had been killed or wounded while three officers and six ratings were captured in this so-called 'scooter raid'. Both Commander Dobson and Lieutenant Gordon Steele, who assumed command of CMB 88 when his captain was fatally injured and went on to sink the battleship, were awarded the Victoria Cross.

From 1922 to 1925, Commander Dobson served with the Royal Australian Navy, before returning to the Royal Navy in the rank of captain. In 1934 Captain Dobson was living with his wife, Edith Archibald MacMechan, and his family at 16 Clarence Road, Walmer, Deal; the family later moving to 16 Archery Square, Walmer. No doubt this old salt, in his retirement, enjoyed looking out over The Downs towards the Goodwin Sands and watching the various vessels entering or leaving the Straights of Dover. He retired from active service in 1935 and was promoted to rear admiral on the Retired List in 1936.

Rear Admiral Claude Congreve Dodson, VC DSO, died in Chatham in 1940 and was buried in Woodlands Cemetery, Gillingham. His medals are on display in the National Maritime Museum.

The War in the Air

The First World War was the first major conflict in which the newly invented aeroplane was to play a major role. It was only just over a decade since 1903 when the Wright brothers had made their historic first flight in a heavier-than-air machine – a flimsy contraption of wood, wire and canvas – and yet soon afterwards aircraft were engaged in bombing, strafing and dogfights over the entrenched troops. A few German planes even carried out bombing raids on England, in some cases inflicting heavy casualties on the civilian population.

But the role of the Allied aircraft was primarily concentrated on the battlefields themselves where, in the early days, they dropped small bombs by hand on the enemy lines and their means of communication. The fitting of Lewis guns to the 'scouts' (as the earlier fighter aircraft were known) led to the shooting down of observation balloons and enemy aircraft and a few skilful pilots on both sides proved themselves very adept and audacious in their exploits.

It was a highly dangerous occupation and the life expectancy of the pilots and their observers was very short, all the more so since the authorities denied them the use of parachutes on the grounds that these might encourage them to jump from a damaged or burning plane rather than sit tight and try to get back to base. Several airmen carried a pistol with the express intention of shooting themselves rather than burn to death in the skies.

A number of Victoria Crosses were deservedly awarded to these brave pioneers of the air although, unlike most of those awarded for valour on the terrestrial or oceanic battlefields, these were more often than not given for brave service in the course of repeated perilous sorties against the enemy. Kent can be proud to be associated with two such remarkable men who justly deserved the highest decoration for gallantry, neither of whom survived the war.

T/Captain James Thomas Byford McCUDDEN

James McCudden was born on 28 March 1895 in the Female Hospital, Brompton, Gillingham, Kent, the third child and second son of Sergeant Major William Henry McCudden of the Royal Engineers. Sergeant Major McCudden was an Irishman, born in Carlow, but his wife, Amelia née Byford, was a Chatham girl whom he undoubtedly met while serving at the School of Military Engineering at Brompton. The family lived at 22 Belmont Road, Gillingham, and at 18 Meyrick Road, Sheerness.

Young James McCudden was educated at the Royal Engineers' School at Brompton Barracks, and later the garrison school at Sheerness, until he was fourteen. Like most young boys from the lower social echelons, this was the age at which he was expected to go out into the world of work and earn his keep, and so James became a Post Office telegrams boy. This employment was brief as, only a year later, he handed in his red bicycle and, aged fifteen, joined the Royal Engineers as a bugler. His elder brother, William, had also joined the army and in 1913 qualified as a non-commissioned pilot, an example to be followed by their younger brother, John.

This life appealed to young James, so he also applied for a transfer to the Royal Flying Corps and, after training, was posted to Netheravon as a mechanic, where his brother gave him several strictly unofficial flying lessons. By the time the war broke out in August 1914, James had qualified as a first-class mechanic and was immediately dispatched to France, where he got his corporal's stripes, advancing to sergeant in April 1915. Shortly afterwards he made his first official flight as an observer and air gunner but it was not until November of that year that he began to fly regularly. It was in May 1915 that he learned of the death of his elder brother, William, in a flying accident while employed as an instructor at Gosport, which affected him deeply. Astonishingly, more than half of all those who volunteered as pilots (8,000 out of 14,000) died in training accidents before they even got their 'wings', and many more lost their lives on active service.

Piloting an aircraft, like driving a car or lorry, was seen very much as a mechanic's job and many potential RFC pilots were given the chance to learn to fly because of their mechanical skills. James tried this route but, unfortunately for him, good mechanics were in short supply and so his application was put on ice. However, he got his chance in January 1916 when he was sent for instruction at Gosport, and qualified as a pilot that April. After a period as instructor, he joined 20 Squadron in France on 4 July, where he flew the rather primitive FE 2d two-seaters on offensive patrols and aerial photography missions. A month later Sergeant James McCudden was posted to 29 Squadron flying DH2 single-seat scouts on offensive patrol and gained his first 'kill' on 6 September, earning him the Military Medal.

On 1 January 1917, James McCudden was commissioned and, later that month, he was shot down for the first and only time in his life. He was unhurt and quickly got back into the air and soon had five victories to his credit, gaining him the Military Cross. His Kentish associations were continued in that year when he was posted to Joyce Green, near Dartford, as an instructor before moving to Dover. He was promoted to temporary captain in June 1917 and was involved in the defence of London against daylight air raids. In August he was posted to 56 Squadron in France as a flight commander, using the superlative SE 5a – the Spitfire of its day. He was supremely successful, shooting down a total of fifty-seven enemy aircraft by the time he left France early in 1918. During this time he was awarded a bar to his Military Cross, the Distinguished Service Order and a bar to the DSO.

McCudden was one of the first really professional airmen, applying a scientific approach to aerial combat. He was fastidious about his guns, his aircraft and his tactics and used his mechanical knowledge to increase the power and ceiling of his machine, enabling him to stalk and destroy the fast and high-flying reconnaissance enemy aircraft. His cool temperament and patience were the keys to his success. As a lone fighter McCudden was without equal and he never lost an opportunity to get a 'kill'. As a flight leader he protected the less-experienced members of his flight, although some claim that he was selfish in 'bagging' targets for himself. The truth would seem to lie somewhere between these two extremes: he usually allowed the experienced members of his team a free rein but kept close control over the less experienced pilots, ensuring their survival.

On 29 March 1918 the twenty-two-year-old Second Lieutenant (Temporary Captain) James McCudden was awarded the Victoria Cross 'for most conspicuous bravery, exceptional perseverance, and a very high devotion to duty'. At the time of the award he had accounted for fifty-four enemy aeroplanes, forty-two of which were destroyed and twelve driven down out of control. On two occasions he totally destroyed four enemy aeroplanes in the same day and, on the second occasion, all four machines were destroyed in the space of an hour and a half. On at least seventy-eight occasions he flew beyond the enemy lines alone, looking for or following enemy aircraft seeking to avoid him.

The following incidents are typical examples of the work he performed. On the morning of 23 December 1917 he encountered four enemy aeroplanes and shot two of them down. That same afternoon, when leading his patrol, he attacked eight enemy aircraft and personally shot two of them down. On 30 January 1918 he single-handedly attacked five enemy scouts, destroying two of them, driving the rest back over their own lines. On 16 February 1918 he destroyed three two-seater aeroplanes during his morning patrol and added a fourth in the afternoon. It was as a result of such exploits that the King considered him deserving of the very highest honour – the Victoria Cross.

Although the French and German authorities had been keen to promote their successful fliers – such as Baron Manfred von Richthofen – as popular heroes or 'aces' in order to foster national pride, the British had been reluctant to follow suit, but now, with the 'press baron' Lord Northcliffe appointed as the Minister of Information and a ready-made hero available, the policy was changed. McCudden's exploits were given a great deal of publicity in Northcliffe's own newspaper, the *Daily Mail*, which asked under the headline 'Our Unknown Air Heroes':

Why an Englishman whose hobby is bringing down Huns in braces and trios between luncheon and tea … should have to wait and be killed before a grateful nation waiting to acclaim him could even learn his name?

Consequently McCudden's details and picture were splashed across the popular press, notably, of course, the *Daily Mail*, and he was widely feted, much to his chagrin. He wrote to a friend:

I see the papers are making a fuss again about the ordinary things one does. Why, that's our work. Why fuss about it? I'm so tired of this limelight business. If only one could be left alone a bit more, and not so much of the hero about it.

With typical modesty, while on leave to collect his VC, the DSO and bar and a bar to his MC from the hands of King George V in London, McCudden 'forgot' to tell his parents. Instead, he went out on the town with Edward Mannock, his rival in the air and, also, it seems, in love, as both pursued an attractive West End theatre dancer called Teddie O'Neill, whom McCudden even took on a joy ride.

To enable McCudden to attend various functions and bolster the government's propaganda, he was posted to Ayr for a period as an instructor, but this and the publicity was not to his liking, and he agitated for a return to France. The authorities were not keen on this because of his high-profile status but his wish was eventually granted and he was appointed to command No 60 Squadron with the rank of major. On 8 July 1918 he flew down to Kent in a brand new SE5a to spend the night with his family and, after breakfasting with his sister, handed her an envelope containing all his medals before taking off for France. Having crossed the Channel, he was unsure of his course, and so landed at Auxi-le-Château to ask the RAF ground crew there for directions to the squadron's base at Boffles. On learning that it was only 5 miles away, he immediately took off once more, but within 90 seconds crashed into a wood adjacent to the airfield. He was taken to hospital but died that evening from a fractured skull and was buried the following day in the British war cemetery at Wavans. It appears that immediately after take-off he made a near-vertical turn, following which the aircraft rolled at low altitude and crashed. Whether this disaster was due to mechanical failure or to pilot error will never be determined definitively.

So ended the tragically short life of the man who has been described as Britain's answer to the German ace, the Red Baron, Manfred von Richthofen – one who respected his opponents and strove continually to hone his own skills: the consummate professional.

Sadly, both his brothers, William and John, also pilots, lost their lives in the war. Their medals, together with those of their father and their brother, James, are on display in the Royal Engineers Museum in Gillingham.

Major Edward MANNOCK

There is something of a mystery about Edward Mannock's early life. It is known that he was born the son of a regular soldier sometime in 1887 (although one book gives 1888). The month was May, but the actual date has been variously recorded as 21 and 24 of that month. Similarly, his place of birth is given as Cork, Brighton and Aldershot. Somerset House has been unable to trace his place and date of birth, suggesting that Cork might be the best bet, as this could account for the lack of record, as the government destroyed the census returns from 1861–1891.

The reason for this uncertainty may also be ascribed to the fact that his Scottish father, Corporal Edward Mannock, was serving in the 2nd Dragoons – The Royal Scots Greys – having enlisted, for reasons best known to himself, under his mother's maiden name. The regiment was based in Aldershot in 1886 and in Brighton in 1887 but it is possible that Mrs Julia Mannock returned to her native Ireland to give birth to her second son, Edward. Mannock himself further confuses the question by giving both Cork and Brighton as his place of birth and varying the date according to his intentions.

Corporal Edward Mannock completed his military engagement but after a short time in 'Civvy Street' he rejoined as a trooper in the 5th Dragoon Guards, this time under his true name. With his new regiment, he went to India, where his wife the three children (Edward being the youngest) joined him and where they remained for seven years, even while newly promoted Corporal Mannock was serving in South Africa. It was during this time that the quiet and reserved Edward first experienced problems with his right eye, believed to have been the result of an amoebic infestation, which bothered him for the rest of his short life.

At the end of the Boer War, Corporal Mannock returned to England, first to Shorncliffe and then to Canterbury, where, in 1901, his family joined him and where Edward Mannock junior's association with the county of Kent began. Corporal Mannock then left the army and the family took up residence in Military Road, Canterbury but shortly afterwards, having been unable to find work, Mannock senior simply upped and left his family, who never heard from him again. Edward was fourteen years old at the time and the family was left penniless.

With no support from the father, the family lived in straightened circumstance and struggled to make ends meet. Edward nevertheless managed to carve out a reputation as a 'capital cricket and football player' (*Kentish Gazette*, 10 August 1918). The family then moved to St Peter's Street from where Edward's elder sister married a soldier. His elder brother was working as a clerk in the National Telephone Company but Edward preferred an outside life and eventually gained employment as a telephone linesman in Wellingborough. In order to keep in touch with his friends down south, Edward joined the Home Counties (Territorial) RAMC, in which he gained the rank of sergeant shortly before 1914.

While in Wellingborough, Mannock lodged with Jim Eyles and his wife, who became lasting friends. Eyles described his lodger in the following terms:

> He was a clean-cut young man, although not what one would call well dressed; in fact, he was a bit threadbare … After he moved in, our home was never the same again, our normally quiet life gone forever. It was wonderful really. He would talk into the early hours of the morning if you let him – all sorts of subjects: politics, society, you name it and he was interested. It was clear from the outset he was a socialist. He was also deeply patriotic. A kinder, more thoughtful man you could never meet.

In early 1914 Edward took a job in Turkey as a telephone engineer with the English Telephone Company but, following the outbreak of the war in which Turkey sided with Germany, he was interned as a prisoner of war. The conditions under which he was confined seriously impaired his health and, because of this, plus his eye problems and his advanced age (he was now nearly twenty-eight – considered rather old for military service), he was eventually repatriated. He returned to England in April 1915 where he promptly rejoined his Territorial unit at Ashford as transport sergeant, understandably harbouring a deep-seated hatred towards his Turkish captors and their German allies.

Mannock soon wanted a more active role in which he would be able to destroy the 'Huns', and so transferred to the Royal Engineers as an officer cadet. The rate of attrition of junior officers by this stage in the war meant that men from the lower social orders who would otherwise have been regarded as 'beyond the pale' were being given commissions and Mannock was very conscious of his humble beginnings throughout the whole of his service.

Once he received his commission he applied to join the Royal Flying Corps and, with the very short life expectancy of flyers in those days, his request was granted. Evidently his eye problem was not seen as too serious, or else the medicals were not very thorough. In August 1916, whilst still at the RE training centre, he received his transfer to the RFC and a posting to the No 1 School of Military Aeronautics in Reading. Although his mother was now living in Birmingham, Mannock gave his address at this time as Rolvenden Layne, Kent.

Moving on to the flying training school at Hendon, Mannock was impatient to get flying and get into the war. He even took a plane without authority and flew off on his own before he had been passed as ready to go solo, an exploit which earned him a 'grounding' by the commanding officer. Mannock was then moved on to the No 10 Training Squadron at Joyce Green, near Dartford, where his instructor was the already distinguished James McCudden (see previous entry).

Mannock did not impress as a natural pilot and consideration was given to returning him to the Royal Engineers. However in November 1916 he passed out and received the coveted RFC wings to sew on his uniform. The following April, with the war little more than a year to run, he received his first operational posting. This was to 40 Squadron on an airfield near St Omer in northern France, the squadron having lost around seven pilots in the past month.

Having accustomed himself to the Nieuport 17 fighter (or 'scout' as they were then known) and the area patrolled by the squadron, Mannock took part in routine patrols and the shooting down of the highly defended observation balloons. Given his future record, it is curious to note that, around this time, he was often criticized by his colleagues as a 'boorish know-all' and for excessive caution – even faint-heartedness – but he watched, studied and learned from his more experienced colleagues and was soon involved in shooting down balloons and dogfights with enemy aircraft. His subsequent exploits may be summed up by the citations for the various decorations he received during the next year or so:

Military Cross – 2nd Lieutenant Edward Mannock, RE and RFC

For conspicuous gallantry and devotion to duty. In the course of many combats he has driven off a large number of enemy machines, and has forced down three balloons, showing a very fine offensive spirit and great fearlessness in attacking the enemy at close range and low altitudes under heavy fire from the ground.

London Gazette, 17 September 1917

Bar to the Military Cross –Captain Edward Mannock, MC RE and RFC

For conspicuous gallantry and devotion to duty. He has destroyed several hostile machines and driven others down out of control. On one occasion he attacked a formation of five enemy machines single-handed and shot down one out of control. On another occasion, while engaged with an enemy machine, he was attacked by two others, one of which he forced to the ground. He has consistently shown great courage and initiative.

London Gazette, 18 October 1917

Distinguished Service Order – T/Captain Edward Mannock, MC RE att'd RFC

For conspicuous gallantry and devotion to duty during recent operations. In seven days, while leading patrols and in general engagements, he destroyed seven enemy machines, bringing his total in all to thirty. His leadership, dash and courage were of the highest order.

London Gazette, 16 September 1918

Bar to the Distinguished Service Order – T/Captain Edward Mannock, DSO MC RE and RAF

For conspicuous gallantry and devotion to duty. In company with one other scout, this officer attacked eight enemy aeroplanes, shooting down one in flames. The next day, when leading his flight, he engaged eight enemy aeroplanes, shooting down the rear machine which broke in pieces in the air. The following day he shot down an Albatros two-seater in flames, but later, meeting five scouts, had great difficulty in getting back, his machine being much shot about, but he destroyed one. Two days later, he shot down another two-seater in flames. Eight machines in five days – a fine feat of marksmanship and determination to get to close quarters. As a patrol leader he is unequalled.

London Gazette, 16 September 1918

Second Bar to the Distinguished Service Order – T/Captain Edward Mannock, DSO MC Formerly Royal Engineers

This officer has now accounted for 48 enemy machines. His success is due to wonderful shooting and a determination to get to close quarters; to attain this he displays most skilful leadership and unfailing courage. These characteristics were markedly shown on a recent occasion when he attacked six hostile Scouts, three of which he brought down. Later on the same day he attacked a two-seater which crashed into a tree.

(The announcement of award of Distinguished Service Order, and First Bar thereto, will be published in a later Gazette.)

London Gazette, 3 August 1918

In the summer of 1918, Mannock had a spell of home leave which he spent with his old friends, the Eyles, in Wellingborough. Jim Eyles later recalled this brief reunion:

I well remember his last leave. Gone was the old sparkle we knew so well; gone was the incessant wit. I could see him wringing his hands together to conceal the shaking and twitching, and then he would leave the room when it became impossible for him to control it. On one occasion we were sitting in the front room talking quietly when his eyes fell to the floor, and he started to tremble violently. He cried uncontrollably. His face, when he lifted it, was a terrible sight. Later he told me that it had just been a 'bit of nerves' and that he felt better for a good cry. He was in no condition to return to France, but in those days such things were not taken into account.

On 5 July 1918, Major Edward Mannock, DSO and two bars, MC and bar, aged thirty-one, arrived at Clairmarais airfield near St Omer to replace the famous Major 'Billy' Bishop as commander of No 85 Squadron. His nerves were obviously beginning to fray but the need for another charismatic leader for this squadron prevailed. However, he showed no sign of any problems on his arrival. One of his pilots, the American Captain Elliot Springs, described how Mannock outlined his aims in a talk to all his pilots shortly after his arrival:

> Mannock has arrived to take charge all rigged out as a major with some new barnacles on his ribbons, and he certainly is keen. He got us all together in the office and outlined his plans and told each one what he expected of them. He is going to lead one flight and act as a decoy ... We ought to be able to pay back these Fokkers a little we owe them.

On 26 July 1918 Mannock was awoken as day broke and made his way to the squadron office before heading out on to the field, accompanied by a young New Zealand colleague, Lieutenant D C Inglis, DCM. Together they climbed into their SE5a machines ready for another dawn sortie, during which Mannock hoped Inglis might get his first 'kill'.

It was a dull, grey day with lowering clouds which meant they would have to fly low but at least they would not have the sun in their eyes. Their destination was the British front line where a couple of German aircraft had been in the habit of harrying the entrenchments. Flying at about fifty feet, they came across a solitary 'Hun' near Lestremme, which Mannock engaged but which Lieutenant Inglis actually shot down – his first kill. The latter takes up the story:

> We circled once and started for home. The realisation came to me that we were being shot at from the ground when I saw the major was kicking his rudder. Suddenly a small flame appeared on the right of Mick's machine, and simultaneously he stopped kicking his rudder. The plane went into a slow right-hand turn, the flame growing in intensity and as the machine hit the ground it burst into a mass of flame. I circled at about twenty feet hoping for the best – but Mannock had made his last flight.

It later emerged that his body had been thrown clear of the plane – or he had jumped clear. There is no evidence that Mannock had carried out his stated intention to shoot himself if his plane caught fire. The body was buried in an unmarked grave by a German soldier who handed in his dog-tags, note books and personal effects. Inglis's own plane was hit but he managed to crash-land just in front of the British lines, from which soldiers came to assist him to safety.

So ended the brief flying career of a remarkable man who, in a very short space of time, had become something of a legend. His DSO and two bars and MC and one bar bear testimony of his bravery and devotion to duty but the list of decorations was ultimately complemented by the supreme award: the Victoria Cross. The *London Gazette* for Friday 18 July 1919 carried the following citation:

His majesty the KING has been graciously pleased to approve the award of the Victoria Cross to the late Captain (acting Major) Edward Mannock, DSO, MC, 85th Squadron Royal Air Force, in recognition of bravery of the first order in Aerial Combat:

On 17th June, 1918, he attacked a Halberstadt machine near Armentières and destroyed it from a height of 8,000 feet.

On 7th July, 1918, near Doulieu, he attacked and destroyed one Fokker (red-bodied) machine, which went vertically into the ground from a height of 1,500 feet. Shortly afterwards he ascended to 1,000 feet and attacked another Fokker biplane, firing 60 rounds into it, which produced an immediate spin, resulting, it is believed, in a crash.

On 14th July, 1918, near Merville, he attacked and crashed a Fokker from 7,000 feet, and brought a two-seater down damaged.

On 19th July, 1918, near Merville, he fired 80 rounds into an Albatros two-seater which went to the ground in flames.

On 20th July, 1918, east of La Bassée, he attacked and crashed an enemy two-seater from a height of 10,000 feet.

About an hour afterwards he attacked at 8,000 feet a Fokker biplane near Steenwerke and drove it down out of control, emitting smoke.

On 22nd July, 1918, near Armentières, he destroyed an enemy Triplane from a height of 10,000 feet. [The citation then gives details of Mannock's previous awards]

This highly distinguished officer, during the whole of his career in the Royal Air Force, was an outstanding example of fearless courage, remarkable skill, devotion to duty and self sacrifice, which has never been surpassed.

The total number of machines definitely accounted for by Major Mannock up to the date of his death in France (26th July, 1918) is 50 – the total specified in the *Gazette* of 3rd August 1918 was incorrectly given as 48 instead of 41.

It is ironic that it was Edward Mannock's errant father, Corporal Edward Mannock, who received his son's Victoria Cross from the hand of King George V. Mannock senior also took possession of his son's other medals and decorations, even though the latter had stipulated that his father should receive nothing from his estate, naming his brother Patrick as his administrator and residual legatee (he left a total of just over £506). The medals were sold soon afterwards for £5 but have since been recovered and are on display in the Royal Air Force Museum in Hendon.

A plaque has been erected in Edward Mannock's memory in Canterbury Cathedral – the city in which he spent much of his young life – and his name was controversially inscribed on the city's war memorial in the Buttermarket. The controversy arose from the fact that Edward Mannock was not born in Canterbury and his connections with the city were limited. However, the *Kentish Gazette* put its weight behind the proposal to include Mannock, the editorial in the issue of 26 July 1919 calling upon the civil authorities 'to do something about recording Canterbury's only VC', stressing that he 'was really a Canterbury product for it was during the years he spent in the city that his fine qualities saw their fullest development, viz. during his boyhood and early manhood'.

The readers of the *Kentish Gazette* were generally in favour of Mannock being recognized as a Canterbury citizen, writing that any failure to act would be a 'lasting disgrace', and so the civic authorities relented.

Chapter 6

The Second World War (1939–1945)

Whereas most of the great battles in the First World War were fought on the Western Front or the Dardanelles, the Army, the Royal Navy and the Royal Air Force were active in numerous theatres of war during the Second World War, several of which are covered in the following pages.

The War in the Air
Out of nearly 1,500 Victoria Crosses awarded since its inauguration, only 51 – a mere 4 per cent – have been awarded to airmen. During the last century many thousands of airmen fought brave battles in the skies, which makes this gallant half-hundred quite a rare breed, and only half of them lived to receive the cherished award in person.

Although the intrepid flyers of the First World War had a not inconsiderable effect on the outcome of the war, it was during the Spanish Civil War that air power showed itself to be the probable deciding factor in future wars, a manifestation which was confirmed during the Second World War. Hitler's plan to invade Britain hinged on the Luftwaffe gaining air superiority before any seaborne incursion could take place and the denial of this during the Battle of Britain effectively caused the invasion plans to be put on hold.

Apart from the dogfights over Kent in the Battle of Britain, the Royal Air Force conducted bombing raids on enemy-held territory, was in action over the North African deserts and over the jungles of Burma, to name but a few places where the roundels of Royal Air Force planes were to be seen – to the delight and relief of Allied troops and civilians and the fear and despair of the enemy.

A/Flight Lieutenant Roderick Alastair Brook LEAROYD
It was during the Battle of Britain, when the RAF had finally begun to make bombing raids over Nazi Germany rather than simply dropping leaflets, that Acting Flight Lieutenant Learoyd set off in his Handley Page Hampden

bomber on a mission which was to earn him one of the first Victoria Crosses of the Second World War.

Roderick Learoyd was a true Man of Kent, having been born on 5 February 1913 at 15 Turketel Road, Folkestone, the son of Major Reginald Learoyd, a Highland Light Infantry veteran of the First World War. The family, of mixed Scottish and Yorkshire descent, had been involved in the Yorkshire textile industry but had settled in Kent living, at the time of the Second World War, in New Romney.

Known to his family as Rod, Roderick Learoyd was educated at Wellington College in Berkshire and the Chelsea College of Aeronautical and Automobile Engineering, following which, at the age of twenty-one, he departed for Argentina, where he spent two years on his uncle's fruit farm. He returned to England early in 1936 at a time when the war clouds were building over Europe and the civil war in Spain was demonstrating the horrors of modern warfare and the importance of air superiority.

Roderick (who became known as 'Babe' to his RAF comrades because of his impressively large size) then took a short-service commission in the RAF and after initial flying training was posted to 49 Squadron, based first at Worthy Down and then at Scampton where in 1938 the squadron was issued with the then-new Hampden bombers. Training continued until the commencement of the war and then, in early 1940, the squadron became involved in small-group daylight bombing raids on strategic targets in Germany and in support of the ground forces before the fall of France.

At 8pm on the night of the 12 August 1940, eleven Hampdens, including six from 49 Squadron, set off from Scampton, their target being the aqueduct carrying the canal over the River Ems, North of Münster. The canal had been raided several times already without much success and was known to be well defended by anti-aircraft guns located on either side of the waterway, creating a gauntlet of fire through which the raiders would have to pass. Four of the bombers were to carry out a diversion while the remaining seven attacked the main target, making their approach at two-minute intervals to ensure the safety of the following bombers. In the event, two of the seven failed to find the target and dropped their bombs elsewhere, leaving just five to attack the canal. Hampden P4403 EA-M, piloted by Flight Lieutenant Learoyd, was scheduled to be the last to drop its bombs and so had to circle the area (or 'stooge around' in RAF parlance) for 10 minutes until all the others had completed their attacks.

The first bomber to make its approach came in at around 100 feet and met with the full force of the flak, was seriously damaged and began to limp home. The second received a direct hit and crashed beside the canal. The third was so badly damaged that it had to jettison its bomb load before climbing to gain enough altitude to enable the crew to bail out safely. The fourth Hampden made a successful run but lost an engine in the process.

It was now the turn of P4403 with Roderick Learoyd at the controls. Flattening out at an altitude of around 150 feet about 3 miles from the target, Learoyd flew straight and level along the canal approach, but by this time 'Jerry had got our range to a nicety, and was blazing away with everything he'd got. The machine was repeatedly hit and ... I was completely blinded by searchlights and had to ask my navigator to guide me in over the target.' At 23.23 hours the bomb aimer/navigator, Pilot Officer John Lewis, dropped the load and the aircraft pulled out of the inferno to a cry of 'Got it!' from the wireless operator. It was subsequently confirmed that the raid had been successful in destroying the target.

A damage control check revealed a number of hits to the aircraft, the most serious of which had ruptured the hydraulic system, but 'Babe' Learoyd nursed the aircraft back to Scampton in the early morning darkness. Since the damage to the hydraulic system affected the undercarriage and flaps, he circled until daylight before setting the battered aircraft down smoothly and safely.

Among the medals awarded to the crews of these hardy aircraft was a Victoria Cross for Learoyd, for having 'repeatedly shown the highest conception of his duty and complete indifference to personal danger in making attacks at the lowest altitudes regardless of opposition'.

It was a popular award as 'Babe' Learoyd was a well-liked and much-respected member of 49 Squadron, renowned for his quiet modesty and cool unflappability. He was given the freedom of the ancient borough of New Romney in November 1940. Following the award he was promoted to squadron leader and in February 1941 became the officer commanding 83 Squadron at Scampton. Further promotion to wing commander in charge of a training unit was followed by the appointment to command 44 Squadron at Waddington – the first squadron to be given the new Avro Lancasters. The remainder of the war was spent either on training duties or with 48 (Dakota) Squadron in West Africa.

Wing Commander Learoyd was demobilized in October 1946 and for most of the rest of his working life he held senior positions with the British Motor Corporation. He had a passion for cars, particularly Aston Martins, and regularly attended the Le Mans 24 hour endurance races and the Silverstone circuit. Wing Commander Roderick Alastair Brook 'Babe' Learoyd never married and died suddenly of a heart attack at his home in Rustington, Sussex on 24 January 1994, just before his eighty-first birthday. His Victoria Cross is held in the Ashcroft Trust collection and his portrait hangs in the Imperial War Museum.

Squadron Leader Robert Anthony Maurice PALMER

The second of the two VCs awarded to Kent airmen went to another bomber pilot. Robert Anthony Maurice Palmer was born in Gillingham on 7 July 1920, the son of Arthur and Lilian Palmer, and was educated at Gravesend Grammar School. On leaving school he was quick to enter the Royal Air Force Volunteer Reserve and was delighted to be called for training as a pilot.

On completion of his elementary and advanced flying training, he gained his 'wings' and flew on his first operation as a bomber pilot in January 1941. The following year he took part in the first thousand-bomber raid on Cologne and was one of the first to drop the four-thousand-pound 'Cookie' bomb. He soon became a very experienced bomber pilot and was one of those selected to join 109 Squadron, forming part of the 8 Group Pathfinder Force. The task of the Pathfinders was to lead the way to a target, usually at low level and often flying the fast De Havilland Mosquito aircraft, and then 'mark' it for the benefit of the main bombing force. By the end of 1944 he had completed 110 bombing missions in every one of which his life, and those of his crew, was in great peril. He was known for his tenacity, high courage and great accuracy and it was only his consummate skill – coupled with a very large portion of luck – that enabled him to complete so many perilous missions against determined enemy flak and night-fighters.

At 10.27 hours on 23 December 1944, when most people's thoughts were concentrated on the approaching festivities, Squadron Leader Robert Palmer DFC and bar, and his crew of six, took off from Little Staughton airfield in Bedfordshire, shortly followed by other Lancaster aircraft from 582 Squadron. His task, as the master bomber, was to locate and pinpoint the target – the marshalling yards at Cologne. Although the RAF usually conducted night raids, this time they were going in daylight, against fearsome odds.

With the enemy fully aware of their approach, the aircraft met with a formidable barrage of anti-aircraft fire, and shortly before reaching the prescribed target Palmer's Lancaster, PB371, was struck. Two of the engines were set on fire and there were flames and smoke in the nose and in the bomb bay. This would have been enough for most men to have abandoned their task and headed for home but Squadron Leader Palmer fully realized the importance of marking the target for the following bombers and so kept a steady course, disdaining any evading action in order to provide an easily seen and accurate aiming point for the others. With the engines developing unequal power, an immense effort was needed to keep the sorely damaged aircraft on a straight course, but, flying at a precise altitude and airspeed and maintaining a steady and straight approach in order to make full use of the 'Oboe' bomb-aiming device, PB371 dropped its bombs right on the target and prepared to leave. But it was too late; the stricken bomber suffered further hits and was last seen spiraling down to earth. Only one member of the crew, Flight Sergeant RK Yeulatt, RCAF, managed to bail out and land safely, to spend the next few months as a prisoner of war. The other six men were all killed in the crash.

Such was the strength of the opposition that more than half the aircraft in the formation failed to return to base. To quote from the citation in the *London Gazette* of 23 March 1945, 'Squadron Leader Palmer was an outstanding pilot. He displayed conspicuous bravery. His record of prolonged and heroic endeavour is beyond praise.' He is buried in the Rheinberg War Cemetery in Germany with the other members of his crew.

The War at Sea

As might be expected, the Royal Navy saw action in all four corners of the globe, both on the high seas under them and, in the case of the Fleet Air Arm, over them. The naval exploits in the North Atlantic, the Far East, on the Russian convoys and elsewhere are well known and do not need rehearsing here. A number of gallantry awards were made to seamen, only one of which has a significant Kent connection. In the event this action took place in the normally peaceful waters of the Mediterranean Sea.

Petty Officer Thomas William GOULD

Tommy Gould was yet another submariner who displayed courage above and beyond the call of duty. He was born at 6 Woolcomber Street, Dover on 28 December 1914 and was only nineteen months old when his father, Reuben Gould, was killed in the First World War. His mother remarried a Petty Officer Cheeseman who was stationed at Dover on the Pilot Cutters and it was perhaps his influence that prompted Thomas, and two of his brothers, to join the Royal Navy.

Thomas Gould enlisted in September 1933 and served in the East Indies on the cruisers HMS *Columbo* and HMS *Emerald*, and later on the China Station. In 1937, aged twenty-three with four years service, he volunteered for submarines, serving on the *Regent*, the *Pandora* and the *Regulus*, being promoted to Acting Petty Officer in 1940. It was around this time that Tommy Gould, on a visit to an old Dovorian friend who had moved to St Albans, met Phyllis Eldridge and was smitten. They married in 1941 and produced a son the following year.

On 16 February 1942 he was the second coxwain on HMS *Thrasher*, patrolling off Suva Bay on the north coast of Crete, when it audaciously torpedoed and sank an enemy supply ship which was protected by no fewer than five anti-submarine vessels. The escorts immediately retaliated, aided by a number of aircraft, dropping a number of bombs and more than thirty depth charges – luckily without damage to *Thrasher*, even though some of them exploded uncomfortably close.

Once darkness had descended over the area, the submarine surfaced to recharge its batteries and, whilst it was still on the surface, loud banging noises were heard when the vessel rolled with the swell, as if something heavy had come loose and was rolling about. An inspection revealed an unexploded bomb lying on the submarine's casing in front of the 4-inch gun mounting. This casing was a light metal free-flooding structure, 3–4 feet high, erected on top of the pressure hull and used to stow a jumble of pipes, wire, ropes and other odd items. The stowage of this gear was Petty Officer Gould's responsibility and so he volunteered to go with the first lieutenant, Lieutenant Peter Roberts, to try to remove the bomb before it rolled off the casing and exploded. Together, the courageous couple ventured forward and wrapped the 100 pound bomb in a potato sack, secured with some rope. The bomb was too heavy and cumbersome for them to throw it clear of the saddle tanks and so they manhandled it some hundred feet to the bows, where they heaved it overboard.

They returned to the casing to see if any damage had been caused and found a jagged hole beneath which they could see another bomb, resting on the pressure hull. If it exploded it would destroy the submarine and they, and the other members of the crew, would be killed by the explosion. Even if it did not explode, the vessel was in enemy waters and, if it were sighted, the captain would have no alternative but to make an emergency dive, and the two men on deck would be drowned. All in all, a very perilous situation.

It was not possible for the two sailors to extract the bomb through the entry hole it had made. The only solution was to bring it up through a hinged metal grating about 20 feet away. Having lowered themselves through the opening, they wriggled on their stomachs past deck supports, battery ventilators and drop bollards to where the bomb lay. Not without difficulty, Gould managed to roll the bomb on to his stomach where he cuddled it like a favourite teddy bear while Roberts lay in front of him, dragging him by the shoulders as he crawled along inside the casing, in places no more than 2 feet high, to the hatch. There they worked the bomb up through the grating, the whole operation taking some 40 minutes, in complete darkness, accompanied by various heart-stopping ticking noises coming from the bomb. Once out of the casing, this second bomb followed the first over the bows.

The two soaked men did not get a heroes' welcome when they re-entered the submarine, the captain, Lieutenant (later Vice Admiral Sir) Hugh 'Rufus' Mackenzie, merely commenting, 'You'd better get yourselves dried.' Indeed, Mackenzie did not make much of the incident in his report and simply commended Roberts and Gould for their 'excellent conduct'.

The Commander in Chief, Mediterranean, Admiral Sir Andrew Cunningham, however, took a more generous view of the incident and recommended both men for the Victoria Cross. Admiral Cunningham's recommendation did not meet with the approval of the Honours and Awards Committee in London, which argued that the deeds were not performed 'in the presence of the enemy' as the Victoria Cross warrant requires, and that the George Cross would be more appropriate. Cunningham's response was that two large enemy bombs on a submarine off the enemy coast was quite enough 'presence of the enemy' and his recommendation was finally accepted.

Petty Officer Gould thus became the Second World War's only Jewish holder of the Victoria Cross, the announcement of the award being made on Mrs Gould's birthday, giving her a delightful and unexpected birthday present. As a VC hero, some years later Gould was asked by the Marquis of Donegal what his thoughts were while he was busy with the bombs. 'I was hoping the bloody things wouldn't go off,' he replied somewhat caustically.

Petty Officer Gould continued to serve throughout the war, experiencing the horror of being trapped on the ocean floor in the Dutch East Indies as well as being bombed by the RAF off Alexandria. But he loved the camaraderie of submarine life and, after being invalided out in October 1945, maintained an interest in the Royal Navy and the Jewish community. He was an Honorary Freeman of Dover and for twenty years the president of the International Submariners Association of Great Britain as well as being an active Mason and involved in Jewish affairs. He was commissioned as a lieutenant in the Royal Naval Reserve and commanded the Sea Cadet Corps in Bromley, where he was then living.

In civilian life he became the personnel manager for the Great Universal Stores catalogue shopping company, but in May 1965, Gould's name was once more in the newspapers, described as the 'VC on the dole'. He had lost his job as personnel managed through a 'clash of personalities' and commented that he was finding his VC a liability.

> Incredible though it may seem, some people in top management seem to shy away from me. I think it might be because they are afraid that a man with such a record could show too much embarrassing initiative. If it is the VC that is frightening people away from me, I wish they would forget it. Those days are over.

Those who knew Tommy Gould described him as a quiet, conscientious man of great personal presence. Meticulous in his habits, he was always smartly dressed, and in later life grew a luxuriant naval beard. On 6 December 2001, after a long illness, Tommy Gould died at the Edith Cavell Hospital, Peterborough, at the age of eighty-seven. His Victoria Cross was sold by Sotheby's in 1987 for £48,400, being purchased by the Association of Jewish Ex-servicemen.

The War on Land

The Second World War was conducted in a number of very diverse theatres, continental Europe, North Africa and South-East Asia being the principal but not the only places where major battles were fought. The loss of the Battle for France, manifested in France's surrender and the ignominious retreat to and evacuation of the BEF from Dunkirk, was followed by a brief period of 'phoney war', leavened only by the equally short-lived battle for Norway. For months the British troops were largely held in the United Kingdom, regrouping, retraining and preparing for the expected invasion of Britain. The first terrestrial military incident that concerns us was the raid on St Nazaire, successful in achieving its aims but regrettable in so far as the casualties were concerned.

Lieutenant Colonel Augustus Charles NEWMAN

Augustus Newman was not a career soldier, unlike many VC recipients, particularly in the nineteenth century. He was born on 19 August 1904 in Chigwell, Essex, the son of Bertram and Margaret Newman, and attended Bancroft's School, an independent boarding school, until he was eighteen. On leaving he joined a small civil engineering firm, WC French, for whom he worked the whole of his civilian life.

He married Audrey Hickman in 1928 and they went on to have five daughters and a son. He had a wide range of interests including rugby, boxing, shooting, music, freemasonry and, especially, golf. He joined the Territorial Army when he was around twenty years of age and never failed to take his clubs with him whenever he went to camp. He first joined the Engineer and Railway Staff Corps but later moved to the 4th Battalion, The Essex Regiment. Although he started as a private soldier, he was soon commissioned, and by the time the Second World War broke out he was a major with some sixteen years experience. The Territorials were soon mobilized and following a period of intensive training Major Newman was asked by his commanding officer if he was prepared to volunteer for a dangerous job. Although he was not given any details, he accepted willingly, eager for some adventure.

And so it was that Newman found himself in command of a motley band of twenty volunteers which, with specialists from the Signals, Engineers and Service Corps, ultimately consisted of around 150 men, forming Number 3 Special Independent Company. These companies, the forerunners of the

Commandos, briefly saw service in Norway where the lack of manpower soon forced evacuation of all the British forces. However, Newman's company had been blooded.

Back in England, the Special Independent Companies reformed and retrained for 'raids on the French coast', although Newman's company was frustrated by being posted to Dungeness on purely defensive anti-invasion duties. For a time Newman thought about asking to rejoin the Essex Regiment who were now in West Africa but he was called to a meeting in Sandwich where it was explained to him that the Independent Companies were to be disbanded and combined into Special Service Battalions and the raiding theme would be carried out on a much larger scale. He willingly accepted the offer to be the second in command of the first battalion to be formed, bringing with him all the men from his old Independent Company.

More intensive training followed, but in April 1941 it was decided that the Special Service Battalions were too large for the type of job envisaged for them and they were to be reformed into smaller units, called 'Commandos'. The 1st Special Service Battalion was to be split into two Commandos, with Newman's old CO in charge of the first and Newman, promoted to lieutenant colonel, the second.

Early in 1942, Newman was called to the War Office where the new Director of Combined Operations, Admiral Lord Louis Mountbatten, informed him that No 2 Commando was to provide the fighting troops for a raid on St Nazaire, the naval side being commanded by Commander RED Ryder. This was more like it! The object of the raid – 'Operation Chariot' – was to render the huge dry dock at St Nazaire unusable by Germany's last remaining battleship, the *Tirpitz*. This was to be accomplished by ramming an old, explosives-packed destroyer into the great dock gates and blowing it up. The job of the Commandos was to land and destroy the pump house and the winding gear for opening and closing the huge caissons.

Inauspiciously, it was on Friday 13 March 1942 that Newman was called back to the War Office and told by Admiral Mountbatten, in no uncertain terms, that he was not expecting anyone to return from this operation. 'If we lose you all, you will be the equivalent of the loss of one merchant ship, but your success will save many merchant ships. We have got to look at the thing in those terms.'

Despite this disquieting news, arrangements for the raid went ahead. The explosives-laden destroyer was an old US vessel, renamed HMS *Campbeltown*, which Newman visited in Portsmouth. He was somewhat surprised at being denied an opportunity to go on board but, as Commander Ryder explained, the sight of a khaki-clad officer boarding her would be of great interest to any Nazi agent who might be watching. The *Campbeltown* was extensively modified to render her similar to a German destroyer, including reducing her four funnels to two and with the main guns and superfluous equipment removed to reduce her draught and enable her to navigate the shallow waters of the Loire estuary. The explosives, consisting of twenty-four depth charges, were located in the original forward gun position and encased in steel and concrete. Lieutenant Commander Stephen 'Sam' Beattie was to be the *Campbeltown*'s skipper. As for the troops, they were to be carried in a fleet of sixteen motor launches which, with the necessary equipment and the naval crew, would be very cramped.

The total complement for the raid was 611 men, of whom 257 were commandos. The commandos were divided into three groups – two in the launches and one on the *Campbeltown* – and further divided into demolition and protection units. Because of the weight of the explosives and other necessary equipment the demolition squad was armed only with pistols but the protection squad was fully armed with Tommy guns, Bren guns and hand grenades. Because the raid would be carried out at night in complete darkness, Colonel Newman instructed his men to scrub their webbing white. They were issued with rubber-soled boots and he told them, 'If you hear anyone whose boots are crunching, you can shoot him – he'll be a German!' A password was required that would be difficult for any German to say, and so the choice fell on 'War Weapons' Week' with the response being 'Weymouth'.

Colonel Newman took a final opportunity to warn his men that there was scant likelihood of their returning from the operation and invited them to stand down should they wish: not one did so. It was planned that the raid would be preceded by a diversionary air raid but Newman's comment – 'I bet you anything you like that the bombing won't work' – proved prophetic. Brought forward by one day because of impending poor weather, the little flotilla set sail from Falmouth on 26 March 1942, escorted by two destroyers, on one of which, HMS *Atherstone*, both Lieutenant Colonel Newman and Commander Ryder sailed.

The crossing was largely without incident and, at 20.10 hours, the flashing signal from the submarine, HMS *Sturgeon*, which was acting as a navigational beacon, was sighted and the military and naval commanders left the *Atherstone* and boarded a motor gun boat (MGB), which led the flotilla for the final leg of the 75-mile journey to St Nazaire. The MGB was followed by the *Campbeltown* with the little troop-carrying launches in single file on either side of her. The escorting destroyers turned away to lay off until the operation had been completed in order to pick up any survivors.

As the assault force entered the Loire estuary the bombing raid began but it was premature and instead of covering the assault merely served to alert the enemy that something was up. The ships were about 2 miles from their target, with the *Campbeltown* flying the German ensign, when they were spotted, caught in a cone of searchlights, and a warning burst of machine gun fire was fired across the *Campbeltown*'s bows. But the raiders were ready for this and a long signal was sent, in German and using the correct call sign, together with a very light recognition signal in order to buy time. Meanwhile the vessels were getting nearer and nearer to their target.

Although the action taken bought the raiders a precious few minutes, the Germans were not stupid and soon realized that all was not as it should be, and opened fire in earnest. The *Campbeltown* went full ahead, began to return the fire and raised the White Ensign instead of the German flag, a gesture copied by the accompanying launches. The forward pom-pom on the MGB managed to silence the harbour defence ship, which was right in the middle of the course the British vessels were to take. The other shore defences concentrated their fire on the *Campbeltown*, which was hit several times, but it continued to steam at its full 20 knots and, at 01.34 hours, just 4 minutes late, she collided with the centre of the massive caisson. Such was the force and speed of the impact that the *Campbeltown* rode up it, coming to rest with her bows on the top of the gate, her 6-hour fuses having been already set.

The stranded *Campbeltown* was not yet done for and she continued to provide covering fire for the commandos who disembarked and made for their respective targets. Headed by the protection units, which quickly silenced four gun positions, the demolition teams made for their objectives and destroyed them within half an hour. While all this was going on Colonel Newman and his HQ staff were put ashore from the MGB, which then began picking up survivors from the *Campbeltown*, while a motor torpedo boat (MTB) fired its torpedoes at the lock gates. Both these little craft then made their way home through the wreckage of the commandos' launches, seven of which had been destroyed before landing their troops, thus drastically reducing the number able to land. In addition a planned landing on the Old Mole had to be abandoned because of the heavy defences there and the commanders of the relevant launches turned around and made their way back to the open sea.

Lieutenant Colonel Newman was unaware of the loss of the launches and the failure to effect a landing on the Old Mole. Making his way around the corner of a building he 'bumped helmets' with a German sentry and instinctively said 'Sorry!' before taking the man prisoner. He set up his HQ behind a building and the remainder of the hundred-odd commandos who had succeeded in landing began to assemble there, the whole time being subjected to withering fire, especially from the fixed gun positions and the ships in the harbour, some of whom were firing at point-blank range. Newman's jovial and cool manner reassured his battered troops and he made for the quayside to arrange for the men to be taken off. It was only then that he appreciated the wholesale destruction of the launches, their wreckage idly floating in water which was itself on fire. 'Well Bill,' he said to his second-in-command, Major Bill Copland. 'There goes our transport.'

With no launches left seaworthy, any hopes of a return to England were dashed and a new strategy had to be formulated. The idea of surrender was quickly discarded, despite the fact that they were nearly surrounded by vastly greater numbers of enemy troops. Newman broke the news to his men in the typically understated terms of 'Well chaps, we've missed the boat home. We'll just have to walk' and broke his command into groups of around twenty men with instructions to try to make their way through the town to the open country beyond, head for Spain and, eventually, Gibraltar, a mere 1,000 miles away!

Still under heavy fire, the survivors made their way to the girder bridge, which they charged across without stopping. The enemy were so surprised at their effrontery that their shots went wide of the mark and they had to pull back, leaving a machine gun nest to be wiped out by the commandos. But the great escape plan was scuppered when several units of the Werhmacht arrived and the route out of town was effectively blocked. Nevertheless, individual small parties began what was later described as the 'St Nazaire Obstacle Race'. To avoid the enemy troops they scrambled through gardens, over walls, through hen houses and even through houses to try to evade capture.

As day broke, Colonel Newman, with about fifteen men, took shelter in a cellar but they were discovered a few hours later. In order to avoid the possibility of them all being killed by a hand grenade, he dashed upstairs and surrendered. They were taken to the German Headquarters where they were joined by other small groups of commandos during the course of the day. Their big worry was that the time for the detonation of the charges on the *Campbeltown* had long past, without anything happening.

The purpose of the raid was puzzling the Germans – so much effort and loss of life for so little. The *Campbeltown* was becoming a great attraction and large numbers of troops and their girlfriends were strolling around on her decks in the sunshine. But, at 10.35am, with a great roar, the *Campbeltown* erupted, causing even more damage than anticipated. Between one and three hundred Germans were blown to pieces, their remains scattered all over the docks. This was followed the next afternoon by further explosions as the torpedoes the MTB had fired at the lock gates also went off.

The prisoners, which now included Lieutenant Commander Sam Beattie and other naval personnel, were taken to a prison camp in Rennes where a German naval officer told Colonel Newman that he wished to bring to his notice the outstanding bravery of Sergeant Tom Durrant (see the next entry) who had continued to fire his Lewis gun, even though mortally wounded.

A move to a camp in Germany followed where the commandant, an old admiral, ordered a special parade. He then asked Newman to bring Sam Beattie before him, upon which he announced that Beattie had been awarded the Victoria Cross. In fact, similar awards to Commander Robert 'Red' Ryder and to Able Seaman Bill Savage were gazetted the same day, but there was no announcement of any award to Newman.

Augustus Newman spent the rest of the war in a prisoner of war camp before being liberated in 1945. On his return to England he put Tom Durrant's name forward for an award and both Durrant and he were awarded the Victoria Cross, the awards being gazetted on 19 June 1945. The citation for Newman continued:

Although Lieutenant Colonel Newman need not have landed himself, he was one of the first ashore and during the next five hours of bitter fighting, he personally entered several houses and shot up the occupants ... utterly regardless of his own safety ... An enemy gun position on the roof of the U-boat pen had been causing heavy casualties to the landing craft and

Lieutenant Colonel Newman directed the fire of a mortar crew against this position to such an effect that the position was silenced. Still fully exposed, he then brought machine gun fire to bear on an armed trawler in the harbour, compelling it to withdraw and thus preventing many casualties in the main demolition area ... By this time, however, most of the landing craft had been sunk or set on fire and evacuation by sea was no longer possible. Although the main objective had been achieved, Lieutenant Colonel Newman was nevertheless determined to try to fight his way out into open country and so give all survivors a chance to escape ... the small force fought its way through the streets to a point near open country where, all ammunition expended, he and his men were finally overpowered by the enemy.

Demobilized, Augustus Newman went back to work for WC French in Essex, retiring as chairman of the now large and prosperous construction company in 1969. His love of golf led him to choose Sandwich for his and Audrey's retirement home and he moved into Fishergate House in that historic old town, close to the famous St George's Golf Club. Sadly he was not to live long to enjoy his retirement and his passion for golf and he died on 26 April 1972 at the age of 67. He was cremated and his ashes scattered in the Garden of Remembrance at Barham Crematorium. His medals are owned by the Ashcroft Trust Collection.

Sergeant Thomas Frank DURRANT

Among the Commandos who took part in the raid on St Nazaire (see previous entry), none distinguished themselves more than Sergeant Thomas Frank Durrant of the Royal Engineers, attached to No 1 Commando, whose bravery prompted the enemy to commend him for an award.

'Tommy' Durrant was born on 17 October 1918 – just before the end of the First World War – in Green Street Green, near Farnborough, Kent. Coming from an honest, working-class family, his early days were generally unremarkable. As a schoolboy he helped out at a local smallholding and was a keen Boy Scout patrol leader. On leaving school he worked as a butcher's boy and later as a builder's labourer but, in February 1937, at the age of 18 he enlisted in the Royal Engineers. After basic training he specialized in explosives and demolition at Shorncliffe camp where his leadership qualities and professional attitude earned him regular promotions.

He was therefore quite an experienced soldier when the Second World War began in September 1939. Anxious to play his part in the struggle and no doubt looking for some excitement he volunteered for the Special Service Independent Companies and went with No 2 Special Independent Company on the ill-fated excursion to Norway in the spring of 1940. It was during his time in Norway that he was promoted in the field to the rank of sergeant.

On the return of the Independent Companies from Norway, and their formation into Commando units, Tommy Durrant found himself in No 1 Commando under Lieutenant Colonel William Glendinning but, when the raid on St Nazaire was mooted, he became attached to Lieutenant Colonel Augustus Newman's No 2 Commando. With the other volunteers he underwent intensive training in Scotland and elsewhere before eventually boarding Motor Launch 306, bound for France, in March 1942.

After a mainly uneventful crossing, the motor launches carrying the commandos began their journey up the River Loire towards St Lazaire and immediately came under heavy fire from German gun positions. Sergeant Durrant was completely exposed in his position abaft the bridge on ML 306 but this did not deter him from returning the enemy fire with the aid of the Lewis gun installed there. Devoid of any cover, Durrant was soon hit, his arm being shattered, but he refused to abandon the gun and continued firing.

A little further down the river the launch was attacked by a German destroyer, the *Jaguar*, at virtually point-blank range and Sergeant Durrant turned his attention to this new threat and fired continuously at the destroyer's bridge, with great coolness and complete disregard for the enemy fire. With the launch illuminated by a searchlight, Sergeant Durrant drew the attention of the enemy guns on himself and was again wounded in several places. Nevertheless, he remained at his post and continued to fire his gun, although by this time he was having to support himself by hanging on to the gun mounting.

The captain of the destroyer, Kapitänleutnant FK Paul, appalled at the way the little launch was suffering and anxious to avoid further loss of life, called upon it to surrender. Durrant's response was a predictable burst of gunfire aimed at the bridge of the enemy ship. By now, growing weaker by the minute from the loss of blood from his many injuries, he continued to direct fire on the enemy, using drums of ammunition as fast as they could be replaced.

A renewed attack by the enemy vessel eventually silenced the fire from the motor launch but Sergeant Durrant refused to give up until the destroyer came alongside and grappled the launch, taking prisoner all the survivors, including the indomitable but seriously wounded Durrant. Indeed, such were his injuries that he died of his wounds the next day in a German military hospital.

Kapitänleutnant Paul was so impressed by the outstanding bravery of Sergeant Durrant that he later sought out Lieutenant Colonel Augustus Newman, VC, the officer commanding No 2 Commando, who had also been taken prisoner, and told him that Durrant should be recommended for the highest possible award in recognition of the way he had conducted himself during the raid. Because all those concerned had been taken prisoner, the recommendation was not made (or was not processed) until the end of the war, and the announcement of the posthumous award of the Victoria Cross to Sergeant Durrant appeared in the *London Gazette* of 19 June 1945, at the same time as that awarded to his commander, Colonel Newman. Tommy Durrant's proud mother received the award from King George VI at Buckingham Palace in October 1946 and it is now held in the Royal Engineers Museum in Chatham.

The body of Sergeant Thomas Durrant VC lies in the cemetery at Escoublac–la–Baule, France.

The Siege of Kohima

The speed with which the Japanese had overrun the Malaya peninsular, followed by the fall of Singapore – the worst military disaster in the history of the British Army – resulted in profound psychological traumas and a long and difficult retreat from Burma.

By March 1944 the battle for Burma had entered its third year and the Japanese, led by the redoubtable Lieutenant General Renya Mutaguchi, prepared to deliver the knock-out blow against the British and Indian troops whom they had so easily vanquished in 1942. The aim of this assault was the annihilation of the British forces at Imphal as a precursor to the invasion of India and the strategy employed was an astute one. Mutaguchi planned to use his 85,000 soldiers to launch a surprise attack on 4 points and, vital to the success of the plan, the village of Kohima, some 5,000 feet up in the Naga Hills, had to be taken. Although he lacked resources, General Mutaguchi believed his troops could live off the land, and was confident that the British defenders would flee in panic, as they had 2 years previously. But he was mistaken on both counts.

The necessary supplies of water, ammunition and artillery and air support failed to materialize, as did the expected reinforcements. In addition, his opponents were no longer the raw, unblooded recruits of yesteryear – under General William Slim they were trained, experienced, disciplined and hardened soldiers. Having just beaten off another Japanese attack in the Arakan, the Anglo-Indian forces were fully prepared and, knowing their likely fate if captured, were ready to fight to the death. And they had the advantage of air supremacy, the newly arrived Spitfires and their pilots proving vastly superior to the tired Japanese Zeros and Oscars.

Nevertheless, the battle for Kohima–Imphal lasted non-stop for 4 months, proving to be the greatest land battle of the entire Pacific theatre. But this was not the only battle: all over the Imphal plain smaller but no less fierce battles were being fought against the Japanese four-pronged assault. Two Victoria Crosses were earned by Kent men in this campaign.

Lieutenant George Albert CAIRNS

Although born in Fulham on 12 December 1913, when he left the Fulham Secondary Central School in Childerley Street, George Cairns went to work in a bank in Sidcup where he met and, in early 1941, married, Ena, who worked for the same bank and they set up home together in that town.

When the war broke out he volunteered for active service and in late 1941 was commissioned into the Somerset Light Infantry. He was later attached to the 1st Battalion of the South Staffordshire Regiment in India and, when that regiment was posted to Burma, he became one of General Orde Wingate's 'Chindits' who harried the Japanese in true Special Forces manner.

On 5 March 1944 Lieutenant (Acting Captain) George Cairns, with other men of the 77 Independent Infantry Brigade (of which the South Staffords formed part), landed by glider at a landing place known as Broadway. A week later the South Staffords and the 3/6 Gurkha Rifles had reached a place known as Henu Block where they set up a road and rail block across the Japanese lines of communication. Early the next day, 13 March 1944, the Japanese retaliated, attacking this position in force and, following some fierce fighting, the South Staffords were ordered to move out and take a hill top from where the enemy attack was being directed.

Lieutenant Cairns took a very active part in this assault, during which he was attacked by a Japanese officer who hacked off Cairns' left arm. Undaunted, Cairns killed his attacker, and, picking up the Japanese officer's sword, continued to lead his men in the attack, slashing right and left with his trophy sword, with which he killed or wounded several Japanese before he himself was cut down. His men were so inspired by this example that the Japanese were completely routed – a rare event.

Grievously injured, Lieutenant Cairns subsequently died from his wounds, but his actions had not passed unnoticed and three of his fellow officers submitted reports to their commanding officer, General Wingate, recommending him for a bravery award. Unfortunately, Wingate was carrying these reports with him when his plane crashed and he was killed, all the paperwork being destroyed. Cairns' regiment forwarded a recommendation to the War Office, only to be told that two of the necessary three witnesses had themselves been killed in Burma, subsequent to the Henu Block action.

The first mention Mrs Ena Cairns had of her husband's outstanding bravery was in 1944 in an airmail letter from his batman, Private N Coales, who wrote, 'He died a hero.' Cairns' commanding officer also paid tribute in a letter. She heard nothing more until late 1948 when the BBC wrote asking her permission to use her late husband's name in a broadcast on famous Midland regiments, which she willingly gave. In December 1948 Cairns' young widow listened to the BBC radio programme and heard, for the first time, the full account of her husband's bravery and the subsequent loss of the citation. She heard the commentator say, 'he fought like a man possessed ... giving Hell to every Jap he could get at, until he dropped unconscious and there he died ... We shan't forget him, ever.'

The programme concluded:

The 'Old Man' recommended him for the VC and the citation was sent home by air with General Wingate. You know what happened – the plane crashed and was lost. So was the citation. And they couldn't find the three witnesses you have to have for a VC; they were all killed or lost.

This was the first Ena Cairns had heard of the citation and she decided to take steps to see that her husband's bravery did not go unremarked. She therefore raised the matter with her MP, Mr GD Wallace, Socialist MP for

Chislehurst who, supported by Brigadier Calvert, pestered the authorities to award the Victoria Cross to this brave officer. Eventually, the award of the Victoria Cross was announced in the *London Gazette* dated 17 May 1949, making it the last VC of the Second World War to be gazetted.

A bronze plaque in Lieutenant Cairns' memory was unveiled at his old school, Fulham Secondary Central School, in Childerley Street, Fulham in July 1950. The bank where he was formerly employed eventually became the Banque Belge Ltd and was very proud of its employee. It too installed a bronze plaque in his memory, which for many years was displayed in the main banking hall. When the building was demolished the plaque ended up in the archives of the Banque Générale in Brussels but, in 1993, it was handed over to the Somerset Military Museum Trust which holds exhibits covering the history of the Somerset regiments, including Cairns' old regiment, the Somerset Light Infantry. His Victoria Cross is on display in the museum of the Staffordshire Regiment in Lichfield.

Lance Corporal John Pennington HARMAN

The other Victoria Cross awarded to a Kent man for his courage in fighting the Japanese in Burma was Lance Corporal John Pennington Harman of the 4th Battalion, the Queen's Own Royal West Kent Regiment. Despite his lowly rank, Harman was not a poor working-class 'squaddie': he came from a wealthy family who owned Lundy Isle in the Bristol Channel, between England and Wales.

John Harman was born in Beckenham, Kent on 20 July 1914, the eldest child of Martin Coles Harman and his wife, Amy Ruth (née Bodger), and was originally educated at Clifton Pre-preparatory School in Bristol but did not settle to school life and discipline there. An ardent nature and animal lover like his father, the sounds of the caged animals in Bristol zoo also upset him, representing as they did 'unwelcome captivity and restraint'. He was therefore delighted when his father moved him to Bedales school near Petersfield in rural Hampshire, which was a haven for non-conformists and allowed him to indulge his love of nature. In 1925 Martin Harman bought Lundy for £15,000 to indulge his passion for the countryside and nature, a decision his young son John wholeheartedly supported.

Just as John was about to leave school in 1931 at the age of 17, his mother died from kidney failure, a catastrophe for John, which was to be compounded by the subsequent bankruptcy of his millionaire father in the

Great Depression. Fortunately he had taken the prudent step of putting Lundy in trust, giving his children a secure base.

These disastrous events turned the whole of John's life upside down and for the next 3 or 4 years he embarked on travels which took him to Spain, South Africa, Australia and New Zealand. John Harman was a somewhat other-worldly person and during his travels he was greatly influenced by an old Spanish sage who introduced him to spiritualism and told him (erroneously) that he would live to the age of 72. This prophecy may have encouraged his utter disregard for his safety in the face of enemy fire in later life.

On his return to England in 1935 he applied to the Air Ministry for a short service commission but was turned down for lack of any qualifications in mathematics. Nevertheless, he gained a Private Pilot's Licence from the Barnstaple and North Devon Aero Club, flying a De Havilland 60 Gipsy I, before settling on Lundy again.

He was 25 when war broke out and so was not immediately called up but in November 1941, perhaps surprisingly given his flying experience, he volunteered for the Household Cavalry rather than the RAF, mistakenly assuming he would be working with animals. What is not surprising, given his background, is that he was more than once offered a commission but steadfastly refused. In fact he heartily disliked army life and its regimentation. In a letter to his father, he wrote:

> I have given the matter of taking a commission a lot of thought and there is no doubt that if I was an officer I would be able to resume the life I was used to, to some extent. On the other hand, I am constitutionally so unsoldierly that I am filled with doubts about the whole thing … Does the status of Gentleman entitle a man to be an officer … though he is not the soldier type? I think not … well!'

His hatred of military life was reflected in his letters home which were a litany of complaints and grouses about the food, the equipment, the boredom, the lack of freedom and, later, the tropical sun.

By the end of 1942 John Harman was still a private soldier, now in the Worcestershire Regiment, but early the next year he was with the 20th Royal Fusiliers and on his way to India. Answering a call for volunteers to transfer to depleted units, John Harman soon found himself in D Company of the

4th Battalion of the Queen's Own Royal West Kent Regiment, 'The biggest blunder of our lives for what we had to go through in Burma' as a fellow volunteer later described it.

In October 1943 the battalion, under Lieutenant Colonel John Laverty, was ordered to move from India to Burma to take part in General Slim's planned offensive. At the end of March 1944, after spending some time in the coastal Arakan region of Burma, the 4th Royal West Kents, comprising 18 officers and 426 men, found themselves settling into billets in the little town of Kohima, 5,000 feet up in the hills.

On 2 April 1944 the Royal West Kents were ordered out to Dimapur, much to the consternation of the Kohima garrison of some 3,000 civilians and non-combattant troops. The Japanese promptly took the opportunity to attack the garrison and forced the outposts back to the main positions. It seemed that the whole of the 31st Japanese Division was about to hit Kohima and so the Royal West Kents moved back up from Dimapur to Kohima Ridge, arriving in the early morning of 5 April. On the way they met stragglers fleeing from Kohima who brought news of the battle that had been raging there for the past few days. The Royal West Kents carried on and, under heavy enemy gunfire, set about re-establishing their positions and digging in on the surrounding hills.

From this moment on the garrison became besieged by a whole division of battle-hardened Japanese troops and fierce, hand-to-hand fighting raged for 3 weeks. On 8 April the remaining road link was blocked and Kohima was completely surrounded by the enemy, who commenced a heavy artillery bombardment.

That evening John Harman, by now a lance corporal, was in command of a forward platoon when under cover of darkness the Japanese set up a machine gun post in a bunker under 50 yards from his own position, which was a serious threat to him and the remainder of his company. The nature of the ground was such that it was not possible to direct the fire of his section on to this machine gun post and so he went forward alone to try to neutralize it. Carrying a hand grenade with a 4-second fuse, to get the maximum effect he released the lever for at least 2 seconds before lobbing it into the post. Entering the post, he ensured that the crew were all annihilated before seizing the machine gun and returning to his own section.

Early the following morning the Japanese attacked the feature known as Detail Hill, which was being held with great difficulty by C Company. Help from D Company was urgently required but it was held down by accurate sniper and machine gun fire from a trench formerly held by C Company further down the slope. Calling out to his men 'Give me covering fire!' Harman fixed his bayonet and alone charged downhill to the post, ignoring the machine gun bullets which peppered his path. A Japanese solider prepared to throw a grenade at him but was shot by Sergeant Tacon with his machine gun. Scrambling up to the edge of the pit, Harman opened fire, shooting four and bayoneting another of the enemy, thereby wiping out the post. Instead of running back to his own position, with his customary insouciance Harman began walking back but his invulnerability for once failed him and he received a burst of machine gun fire in his back.

His company commander, Major Easten, risked his own life and crawled out of his trench to bring Harman in, calling for stretcher bearers but Harman, still conscious, said, 'Don't bother Sir … I got the lot. It was worth it,' and died in Easten's arms.

Lance Corporal Harman's bravery and self-sacrifice inspired many a faint heart to fight on with renewed determination and the resistance continued until a relief column arrived on 18 April. As Major Easten recorded:

> We must have presented a strange spectacle. Bearded, filthy men with glazed eyes who had not slept for fourteen days (we all slept a little I suppose, but mainly standing up). Wounded, with filthy bandages and pale, grey faces, and weak but cheerful grins … But the greatest honours are due to Tommy Atkins … He fought hand-to-hand battles practically every night and his pals were shot down all around him. If he was wounded he had no hope of evacuation. Day after day he was promised relief that never came and his platoon or section or just 'gang' got smaller and smaller.

The regiment lost 61 killed, 13 missing and 125 wounded but accounted for more than 250 of the enemy. One private soldier, being the sole remaining member of his platoon, cheekily asked if that made him an acting second lieutenant!

A tribute to Lance Corporal John Pennington Harman's self-sacrifice, and that of many like him, is made on the Kohima memorial that poignantly records:

> When you go home, tell them of us and say;
> For your tomorrow, we gave our today.

John's father, Martin Coles Harman, had a stone memorial built to his son's memory on Lundy Isle, which was unveiled at a ceremony in the presence of Colonel John Laverty and several other West Kents, including Sergeant Tacon, the machine gunner who had saved John's life and slaughtered the Japanese as they ran from Detail Hill. Martin Harman never spoke of his son to his other children but he carried John's Victoria Cross with him for many years and would proudly show it to complete strangers. The Cross is now held in the Royal West Kent Regiment Museum in Maidstone.

In his lifetime Martin Harman was very keen to avoid Lundy being called 'Lundy Island' as the name is Norse for Puffin Island; therefore the word 'island' is tautologous. The island is now owned by the National Trust and generally referred to as Lundy Island.

T/Major William Philip SIDNEY

William Philip Sidney was born in Chelsea on 23 May 1909, the younger of two children, and the only son of William Sidney, 5th Baron de L'Isle and Dudley, a barrister and politician. He was educated at Eton College and Magdalene College, Cambridge, although he was apparently more interested in sports and the Officers' Training Corps than academic matters. On coming down from Cambridge in 1929 he was commissioned as a second lieutenant in the Grenadier Guards' supplementary reserve of officers, but continued to work in the City of London, where he qualified as a chartered accountant. He developed a great love of country life and in his spare time liked nothing more than to help his father manage the extensive family estates at Penshurst Place, near Tonbridge, and Inglesby Manor at Great Ayton in Yorkshire.

When the Second World War broke out in 1939 William Sidney held the rank of captain and, joining his regiment, served with the BEF in France, being one of the last to be taken off the beach at Dunkirk in May 1940 under heavy air attack. Very soon after his return to London he married Jacqueline Vereker, the only daughter of John Vereker, the Viscount Gort VC, under whose command he had served in France. They had four daughters and a son.

The so-called 'phoney war' was spent training in commando tactics, following which his regiment was posted to North Africa. He held the rank of temporary major and was in command of a company of the 5th Battalion of the Grenadier Guards when they landed on the Anzio beachhead in Italy on 22 January 1944. This landing, commanded by the American General John P Lucas, was conceived to outflank the German forces and open the way for an attack on Rome. The success of an amphibian landing at this point, in a marshy basin surrounded by mountains, depended entirely on the element of surprise and the swiftness with which the invaders could move, relative to the time needed for the defenders to react and occupy the mountains thus entrapping the invaders. Unfortunately General Lucas appears to have failed to appreciate this requirement and, following a virtually unopposed landing and occupation of the general area, he decided to consolidate and dig in pending the arrival of reinforcements and further supplies. A jeep patrol actually reached the outskirts of Rome without meeting any resistance but, despite this news, General Lucas failed to push on and threw away the element of surprise, giving the enemy commander, General Kesselring, the opportunity to move every spare unit he had into the ring around the beachhead. As a result, instead of enjoying a walkover, the invading troops were met with fierce resistance. In the words of Winston Churchill, 'We hoped to land a wildcat that would tear out the bowels of the Boche. Instead, we have stranded a vast, beached whale with its tail flopping about in the water.' After a month General Lucas was relieved of his command and replaced by General Truscott.

The period between 6 and 10 February 1944 – some 2 weeks after the successful landings – was of critical importance to the whole state of the Anzio beachhead. The Germans attacked a single British division with units from six different divisions, resulting in ferocious localized hand-to-hand battles, each of which had an immediate effect on the position of other, neighbouring units and on the action as a whole. It was essential that every inch of ground should be fought for in a dogged and stubborn manner. The Carroceto-Buonriposo Ridge was particularly important.

During the night of 7–8 February, Major Sidney was commanding the support company of the Grenadier Guards, his headquarters being located to the left of the battalion headquarters in a gully to the south west of the Carroceto bridge. German infantry had skirted the forward rifle company to the north west of the town and made a strong assault near Major Sidney's company HQ and managed to penetrate into the wadi. Major Sidney gathered up the crew of a 3-inch mortar which was busy firing at the approaching enemy and personally led an attack, using hand grenades and Tommy guns, and drove the Germans out of the gully. He then ordered the crew back to resume firing their mortar while he and a handful of other soldiers manned positions on the edge of the gully in order to repel any further attack. This small detachment was successful in keeping most of the enemy out but a few Germans managed to reach a ditch just 20 yards in front of the defending guardsmen, which would enable them to outflank the defence. In full view and completely exposed, Major Sidney dashed forward to a point from which he could engage the enemy with his Tommy gun at point-blank range. He killed a number of them and the remainder rapidly withdrew.

Returning to the gully, Major Sidney kept two guardsmen with him and sent the rest back for more ammunition and hand grenades. It was during this absence that the enemy suddenly renewed their attack and a grenade struck and injured the major's face before bouncing off and exploding. Both the major and one of the guardsmen were injured and the second man was killed. Single-handed and despite a further painful wound to the thigh, Major Sidney kept the enemy at bay for 5 minutes until the ammunition party returned and drove the enemy off.

Once he was satisfied that no further attacks were likely, Major Sidney started to make his way to the aid post to have his wound dressed, but, before this could be done, there was another attack on his position. He at once returned to the scene and continued to fight off the enemy for another hour, by which time the battalion's position was consolidated and the Germans finally driven off. Only then, weak from loss of blood and scarcely able to walk, did Major Sidney consent to have his wounds attended to.

With the coming of daylight it was anticipated that he would be able to move to the rear for proper medical attention but fighting continued along the front and it was not possible to evacuate him until that night. Nevertheless, throughout this time and in considerable pain, Major Sidney continued to encourage and inspire those around him. His action the previous night, in the face of considerable odds, enabled the battalion to re-establish its position with far-reaching consequences for the battle as a whole.

Major Sidney's wounds were such that he was invalided out of the army and transferred to the regular army reserve before receiving the Victoria Cross at the hands of King George VI in October 1944. This was accompanied by a piece of VC ribbon taken from the tunic of his father-in-law, Lord Gort. Only 2 days later he was returned unopposed as the Conservative Member of Parliament for Chelsea in a by-election. His career in the Commons was cut short in June 1945 when he succeeded to the peerage on the death of his father and entered the House of Lords as the 6th Baron de L'Isle and Dudley.

Although active in the Lords, he also worked in the City of London, and spent a great deal of time maintaining and improving his historic country seat and gardens at Penshurst Place, the former home of his Elizabethan forebear, Sir Philip Sidney. When the Conservatives were returned to power in 1951, de L'Isle and Dudley was appointed Secretary of State for Air by Churchill and showed his determination to be a 'hands-on' appointee by learning to fly at the Royal Air Force Central Flying School and becoming the first air minister to fly a jet aircraft (a Canberra). During his tenure, the Royal Air Force more than doubled in strength.

In January 1956 he was created the first Viscount de L'Isle, dropping the 'Dudley' from his title, and in August 1961 was appointed the last English Governor General of Australia. He returned to England in September 1965 and, his wife having died in 1962, remarried Margaret Eldrydd, Lady Glanusk in March 1966 and set up home at Penshurst Place.

Viscount de L'Isle, 'a brave and distinguished nobleman' (*The Independent*, 13 April 1991), died at his beloved Penshurst Place on 5 April 1991, being survived by his second wife and the five children from his first marriage. His son, Major Philip John Algernon Sidney (b1945), succeeded to the title.

Captain Lionel QUERIPEL

Among the outstanding battles of Second World War, 'Operation Market Garden' – the airborne attack on occupied Holland in September 1944 – must rank among the best known and most revered. The largest airborne operation of all time, its objective was to seize the bridges across the Meuse River and the two Rhine tributaries, the Waal and the Lower Rhine, as well as several smaller waterways. This would permit armoured units to advance rapidly into Northern Germany and open up Germany's industrial heartland, the Ruhr.

At first all went well and several bridges between Nijmegen and Eindhoven were secured but at Arnhem the British 1st Airborne Division met with unexpectedly strong opposition. In the end a small force managed to hold one end of the Arnhem road bridge but the failure of reinforcements to get through led to them being overrun on 21 September. The rest of the division were cornered in a small pocket to the west of the bridge and had to be evacuated on 25 September. As a result, the Allies failed to cross the Rhine in sufficient numbers and it remained a significant barrier until the following spring. Among the British troops there was one young captain who was to distinguish himself amongst this illustrious company and gain the Victoria Cross.

Lionel Queripel was born in Wiltshire on 13 July 1920 but when he was six the family moved to 52 Warwick Park, Tunbridge Wells, which became his home from then on. Lionel came from a well-established and highly decorated military family. His father, Colonel LH Queripel, had taken part in the action to put down the Boxer rebellion in 1900 and later served in Mesopotamia, France and Russia during the First World War, gaining a DSO and CMG on the way. His grandfather and great grandfather also served with distinction in Queen Victoria's army.

Following his education at Marlborough College, and in accordance with the family tradition, Lionel joined the army in 1939, just before the outbreak of the Second World War, and was commissioned in the 2nd Battalion of the Royal Sussex Regiment. The 2nd, 4th and 5th Battalions were sent to France in 1940 as the 133rd (Royal Sussex Regiment) Brigade and the survivors were among those rescued from Dunkirk. The 2nd Battalion then went to North Africa where it suffered heavy casualties in the Battle of El Alamein in 1942. Reforming in Kabrit in the Suez Canal Zone after the battle, it was decreed in January 1943 that the battalion, together with volunteers from the 4th and 5th Battalions, should be converted to a parachute unit under Lieutenant Colonel KBI Smyth of the South Wales Borderers. Some 200 men volunteered for parachute training and these formed the basis of the 10th Parachute Battalion.

The newly formed parachute battalion saw service in Italy for a short time before returning to England to take part in the preparations for D-Day. In fact, the battalion did not go to Normandy, but remained in Great Britain until Operation Market Garden when, on 18 September 1944, it jumped in the second airlift near Arnhem, facing heavy enemy fire. The aircraft in which the A Company commander was flying was shot down south of the Rhine and so Captain Queripel, as the second in command, took charge of the company.

The next day the 10th Battalion's advance along the main Amsterdamseweg road was held up by a strong German force at its junction with the

Driejenseweg and a battle using both rifle and mortar fire ensued and lasted for several hours. A Company had been only marginally involved in this action but Queripel then received orders to mount a wide flanking attack. The company was almost immediately subjected to heavy fire, causing it to split on either side of the embanked road, suffering considerable losses. Captain Queripel set about reorganizing his force, crossing and re-crossing the road under extremely heavy and accurate fire. At one point he carried a wounded sergeant to the Regimental Aid Post and was himself wounded in the face while doing so.

Having managed to regroup his troops, Captain Queripel personally led an attack against a strong point where German troops, armed with a captured British anti-tank gun and two machine guns, were holding up the advance. Despite the fire directed at him, Queripel killed both machine gun crews and recaptured the anti-tank gun, thus enabling the advance to continue. The flanking movement proved unsuccessful, however, and little ground was gained in what was to be the final attacking action of the 1st Airborne Division at Arnhem.

During that evening, whilst the 4th Parachute Brigade was in the process of transferring its vehicles through a tunnel under the railway line, Captain Queripel was given the command of a composite company, consisting of his own A Company plus men from the remnants of two other battalions. With this motley but courageous band, Queripel was to hold a small finger of woodland less than a quarter of a mile from the tunnel. This point was vital to the defence of the remaining paratroopers and, as such, was pressed very hard by the Germans throughout the night. The next day, finding himself cut off with a small party of men, Queripel took up position in a ditch and despite having received further wounds to both arms and being subjected to heavy mortar and Spandau fire he continued to inspire and encourage his men to resist with hand grenades, pistols and the few remaining rifles.

As the pressure increased, Captain Queripel decided that it was impossible to hold the position any longer and ordered his men to withdraw. Despite their protests, he insisted on remaining behind to cover their withdrawal with his automatic pistol and a few hand grenades. He was never seen again. The rest of the battalion fought to virtual annihilation in the besieged Oosterbeek sector with only a handful of survivors escaping across the Rhine.

The citation for the Victoria Cross concluded:

During the whole period of nine hours of confused and bitter fighting Captain Queripel displayed the highest standard of gallantry under the most difficult and trying circumstances. His courage, leadership and devotion to duty were magnificent and an inspiration to all.

Lionel Queripel's remains lie, with many of his comrades, in the Arnhem Oosterbeek War Cemetery in the Netherlands.

Captain John Henry Cound BRUNT

John Brunt first saw the light of day on 6 December 1922 in the village of Priest Weston, Shropshire, being born into a farming family. His father was Thomas Henry Brunt and his mother Nesta Mary, née Cound (hence the unusual forename), and he had two sisters, Dorothy and Isobel. When he was six the family moved to a farm near Whittington (Shropshire) where he grew up and began to show signs of the daredevil nature which was to stand him in good stead in later life. On one occasion he took off all his clothes and jumped into the Shropshire Canal because he wanted to learn to swim. On another occasion he was found swinging himself along the shaky guttering of a Dutch barn sixty feet above the farmyard.

Once he was old enough, he was enrolled as a boarder at Ellesmere College, where he continued to demonstrate his mischievous streak by slipping a laxative in the matron's tea and his sporting prowess by playing cricket, hockey, rugby, water polo and wrestling. It was while at the college that he caught measles, which led to him needing glasses for the rest of his short life.

In 1934, when John was 12, the family moved to Paddock Wood in Kent where, when not at school, 'Young John' as he was known in the village made himself popular helping with the hop-picking and later, when war was declared, helping to train the Paddock Wood Home Guard.

In 1941, at the age of 18, he enlisted in the Queen's Own Royal West Kent Regiment as a private soldier, but a little more than a year later he was commissioned as a second lieutenant in the Sherwood Foresters and posted to North Africa. However, although commissioned into the Sherwood Foresters, he never served with them. On the boat to Africa he chummed up with Captain Alan Money, an officer with the Royal Lincolnshire Regiment, and so arranged to transfer to the 6th (Territorial) Battalion of that county regiment.

Lieutenant Brunt's stay in Africa was a short one as on 9 September 1943 his battalion took part in the landings at Salerno on the south west coast of Italy, which had the intention of taking Naples, some 30 miles to the north. The landings met with fierce opposition from the German defenders (who were in the process of taking over from the defeated Italians) and the invading force was unable to break out from its shallow beachhead for some time.

Lieutenant Brunt was in command of No 9 Platoon in A Company and, from December of that year until the following January, he was in command of a battle patrol which was constantly involved in action. On 15 December 1943 he was given orders to eliminate an enemy post based in some houses on the northern bank of the River Peccia. Seeking a way through the enemy lines, he crossed and re-crossed the river so many times that his men began calling it 'Brunt's Brook'. Eventually Brunt led a section in an assault on the houses. There was little resistance from the first two but the third contained a number of battle-hardened members of the crack 2nd Herman Goering Panzer Grenadier Regiment. After half an hour's stiff fighting, with one of his men killed and six wounded, Brunt ordered his patrol to withdraw but he remained with two others to retrieve a wounded comrade. This action earned him the Military Cross.

In March 1944 the 6th Battalion of the Lincolnshire Regiment was taken out of the line and moved to Egypt and Syria to reform and refit having lost 518 men. The battalion went back to Italy in July 1944 with John Brunt newly promoted to the rank of temporary captain and appointed the second in command of D Company. By the end of the year the battalion was deployed near Ravenna and was busily engaged in harassing the enemy who were retreating northwards through Italy. On the night of 3 December the battalion commenced an attack on the German-occupied town of Faenza and 3 days later had taken the town and set up defensive positions there.

At dawn on 9 December 1944, Captain Brunt's platoon was holding a vital sector of the line when the 90th Panzer Grenadier Division made a strong counter attack on the forward positions, using tanks and infantry. The house around which the platoon was dug in was destroyed and the whole area subjected to intense mortar fire. With the anti-tank defences destroyed and two Sherman tanks knocked out, the situation became critical. Captain Brunt, however, rallied his remaining men and, moving to an alternative position, continued to hold the enemy infantry at bay, although outnumbered by at least three to one. Firing a Bren gun, Captain Brunt personally killed around fourteen of the enemy. His wireless set was destroyed by enemy shell fire but when he received a message by a runner to withdraw to a company position some 200 yards to his left and rear, he remained behind to give covering fire. When the ammunition for his Bren gun ran out he used a PIAT (projectile infantry anti-tank) missile launcher and a 2-inch mortar that casualties had left behind before finally dashing over the open ground to the new position. His aggressive defence caused the enemy to pause, so during a brief lull in the fighting Captain Brunt took a party back to his previous position and, although subjected to small arms fire, carried away the wounded who had been left there.

Later the same day the enemy made a further counter attack on two axes and so Captain Brunt seized a spare Bren gun and, going round his forward position, rallied his men. Then, leaping on to a Sherman tank which was supporting the company, he directed the tank commander to drive from one firing position to another, all the time sitting or standing on the turret, directing fire at the advancing enemy, regardless of the hail of small arms fire. Then, seeing small parties of the enemy, armed with bazookas, trying to approach round the left flank, he jumped off the tank and, taking a Bren gun, stalked these parties well in front of the company positions, killing more of the enemy and finally causing them to withdraw in great haste, leaving their dead behind.

The next morning, having won the battle and the acclaim of his regiment, Captain Brunt was eager to return to the offensive and was keeping alert for further trouble while breakfast was being prepared for his men, which would be their first meal for 48 hours. He was standing in the doorway of the platoon headquarters, drinking a mug of tea and chatting with friends, when a stray German mortar bomb exploded at his feet, killing him outright. It was just 4 days after his 22nd birthday.

The citation for the award of the Victoria Cross, published in the *London Gazette* on 8 February 1945, concluded with the following encomium:

Wherever the fighting was heaviest, Captain Brunt was always to be found, moving from one post to another, encouraging the men and firing any weapon he found at any target he could see. The magnificent action fought by this officer, his coolness, bravery, devotion to duty and complete disregard for his own personal safety under the most intense and concentrated fire was beyond praise. His personal example and individual action were responsible to a very great extent for the successful repulse of these fierce enemy counter-attacks.

In December 1945, the war now completely over, John Brunt's father, Thomas Brunt, received his son's Military Cross and Victoria Cross from King George VI. On meeting Field Marshal Alexander at the ceremony, Thomas Brunt said to him, 'I expect you know many men who should have been awarded this medal.'

The Field Marshal replied, 'No, because there is always only one who will do the unexpected and on that day it was your son.'

Paddock Wood was very proud of its local hero and on 3 September 1947 – exactly 8 years after the declaration of the war – the Kent Arms public house in the village, which had been John Brunt's 'local', was renamed John Brunt VC in his honour by the brewers and owners, Whitbread Ltd. Half a century later, the pub having fallen into disrepute for drugs, disturbances and after-hours drinking, it was sold to the Hooden Horse Inns chain of public houses who, in accordance with their policy, changed the name to The Hopping Hooden Horse, first part of the name being in recognition of the fact that the village was the centre of the West Kent hop industry. Responding to numerous letters of complaint, the new owner responded, 'All our pubs contain the corporate Hooden Horse name and there was simply no way we could have made the place work under the name John Brunt VC.'

The villagers were furious and many boycotted the pub and there were great sighs of relief when in June 2001 new owners arrived and decided to revert to the previous name. The original pub sign disappeared during the earlier renovations and so a new one was commissioned and now proudly hangs outside this popular watering hole.

Lance Corporal Henry Eric HARDEN

Although several medical men have been awarded the Victoria Cross over the years – usually medical officers – only one was awarded during the Second World War and this to a lowly lance corporal in the Royal Army Medical Corps.

The war was drawing to a close in January 1945 but there was still bitter fighting over many fronts in Europe as the Nazi forces fought a fierce rearguard action against the Allied troops pressing them back towards the Fatherland and to Berlin. Among those closely involved in this final push was

Eric Harden, a lance corporal in the Royal Army Medical Corps, attached to 45 Royal Marine Commando.

Eric Harden was born on 23 February 1912 at Northfleet, Kent, the seventh son of a family of eight. He proved himself to be a keen sportsman, excelling at tennis, football and swimming. He also played the violin. Right from the early age of 10, Eric helped out in his brother-in-law's butchers shop, taking over the shop when his brother-in-law died just as Eric was old enough to leave school. In his spare time he also developed an interest in medical matters and joined the St John's Ambulance Brigade. In 1936 he married Maud Pullen and they had a son and a daughter.

Not a natural soldier, Eric was 30 before he was conscripted into the Royal Artillery in 1942. However, his medical training and experience was noted, and he was soon transferred to the Royal Army Medical Corps, serving with a Field Ambulance section. Unhappy with the routine and inactivity of service in Great Britain, he volunteered for attachment to the Commandos, and was appointed a medical orderly with A Troop of 45 Royal Marine Commando.

In June 1944 45 Royal Marine Commando took part in the Normandy landings and found itself fighting its way through the Norman *bocage* in the Merville area, where Harden was kept busy tending the wounds of his injured colleagues. Eventually 45 Commando was recalled to England for replacements and refitting in anticipation of a posting to the Far East. However, in January 1945 the unit was instead ordered to return to north-west Europe and Lance Corporal Harden soon found himself near the village of Brachterbeek in the Netherlands.

On the freezing morning of 23 January, A Troop had been given the task of taking the village railway station. As they moved across the open towards their objective, the leading section of the troop came under heavy fire from machine guns, mortars and artillery as soon as it reached a crossroads, isolating it from the rest of the command. Because of the lack of cover, the section moved into some houses along the Stationsweg but, in doing so, lost a number killed or wounded. Jeeps sent out to retrieve the injured men under the protection of a Red Cross flag were fired upon as they returned, in blatant breach of the Geneva Convention, one being completely destroyed and all the occupants killed.

Despite this clear indication that the enemy were not prepared to give quarter to the injured, Harden scuttled 100 yards across open ground to render first aid to three marines, including the section commander,

Lieutenant Corey. Then he heaved one of them on to his back and carried him to the medical aid post that had been set up in one of the houses. He himself received a slight wound to his side during this exploit and was instructed not to go out again, while attempts to retrieve the casualties were made using tanks. This proved unsuccessful due to accurate anti-tank fire from the enemy positions, and a further attempt using a smokescreen simply increased the enemy fire directed towards the casualties. Harden therefore insisted on going back to rescue the remaining two commandos, taking two stretcher-bearers with him. They succeeded in getting one more man out but he was hit again and died as they did so. The gallant trio then went back again to extricate the remaining casualty, Lieutenant Corey, and it was whilst doing so that Lance Corporal Harden was shot in the head and killed instantly. The stretcher party returned safely to their unit's position but Harden's body had to lie in the open until the next day.

Harden's actions during this long period of time were directly responsible for saving the lives of the wounded men he brought in and there is no doubt that this had a steadying effect on the other troops in the area at a most critical time. The Victoria Cross citation concluded:

His complete contempt for all personal danger and the magnificent example he set of cool courage and determination to continue with his work, whatever the odds, was an inspiration to his comrades and will never be forgotten by those who saw it.

Lance Corporal Harden is buried in the Commonwealth War Graves Commission cemetery in Nederweet, Limburg, Holland. There are two stone plaques, one in English and one in Dutch, in the village of Brachterbeek to commemorate his action. An earlier bronze plaque installed in 1947 was stolen in 1965.

The Victoria Cross, awarded posthumously, was presented to his widow, Maud, by King George VI on 9 April 1946 and is now on display at the Army Medical Services museum in Aldershot.

Lieutenant George Arthur KNOWLAND
Only a week after the action that won Henry Harden the Victoria Cross in Holland, another Kent man won the same award in Burma. George Arthur Knowland was born in Catford on 19 August 1922 and, following the death

of his mother, he spent some time in an orphanage as being 'in need of care and protection'. He later lived with his father in Croydon and attended a local school there before enlisting in the army in 1940 at the age of 18. He first joined the Royal Norfolk Regiment as a private soldier but later volunteered for the Commandos. After training he fought with distinction with No 3 Commando in Sicily and Italy and was promoted to the rank of sergeant. Selected for officer training, he returned home, where he married Ruby Weston.

In January 1945 the newly commissioned Lieutenant Knowland was posted to the Far East to join No 1 Army Commando in Myebon, Burma, as a section leader in No 4 Troop. No 1 Army Commando had fought in North Africa and taken part in the Torch Landings but for some time now had been training in India for the assault on the Arakan Peninsular. Together with their comrades in No 5 Army Commando and 44 and 42 Royal Marine Commandos, they were ordered to take and hold the dominant features of the southern Chin Hills in order to cut off the supply and escape routes of the Japanese and to secure the bridgehead. The objective for No 1 Army Commando was a feature referred to as Hill 170 (code named 'Brighton'), which they duly took and dug in, with No 4 Troop being given the task of defending the most northerly end of the hill. Lieutenant Knowland's platoon had the unenviable task of manning the Troop's forward position.

This episode quickly turned into an epic battle, during which, on 31 December 1945, an estimated 700 artillery shells fell on the hill on which the Japanese commander had decided to concentrate his numerically superior force of around 300 men. The first assault was aimed in particular on the area defended by the twenty-four survivors of Knowland's platoon and there followed continuous battles, much of it hand-to-hand, in the course of which the commandos succeeded in repelling and counter attacking the waves of fanatical Japanese.

The newcomer, Lieutenant George Knowland, was prominent among the defenders, his courage and energy being an inspiration to all around him. Moving from trench to trench, he encouraged and emboldened his men, using whatever weapons came to hand: rifle, grenades, light machine gun. When all the crew of one of his forward Bren guns had been wounded, he manned the gun himself until a fresh crew came up from the troop headquarters. The attacking Japanese were in dead ground, just 10 yards away, and so standing up in full view on top of the trench in order to get a better field of fire, Lieutenant Knowland sprayed the attackers with bullets until they fell back, enabling the medical orderly to treat the wounded crew. The replacement crew became casualties on the way up so Knowland continued to hold the position until yet another crew arrived.

Despite thus making himself the target for heavy enemy fire, he miraculously escaped unhurt until a further enemy wave came close to overrunning the position. Then, when the attack came in, he took a 2-inch mortar and, highly dangerously, fired it from the hip, resting against a tree stump, killing six of the enemy with his first bomb. When he ran out of ammunition, he went back through heavy grenade, mortar and machine gun fire, to get more which he fired in the same manner in the open, in front of his platoon. When these bombs were finished he went back to his own trench to fire his rifle at the enemy. Being hard pressed and with the enemy closing in on him from only 10 yards away, he had no time to reload his rifle's magazine, and so he grabbed a Tommy gun from an incapacitated comrade and sprayed the enemy with this. At this very moment of victory he was mortally wounded, but not before he had accounted for a large number of the enemy.

Such was the inspiration of his heroism that although fourteen of his platoon of twenty-four men became casualties at an early stage and six of his positions overrun by the enemy, his men held on through 12 hours of fierce and continuous fighting until relieved. Had this northern end of the hill fallen, the whole position would have been endangered and the beachhead dominated by the enemy with other units inland cut off from supplies. In the event, the defenders lost no ground and the critical position was held until reinforcements arrived. Scattered around Hill 170 there were 2,300 dead Japanese while in front of the forward positions held by No 4 Troop alone there lay the bodies of 340 of the enemy. Shortly afterwards a successful counter attack was launched by Allied troops from the vital ground that Lieutenant Knowland had taken such a gallant part in holding in the face of overwhelming odds.

George Knowland's body was buried at Taukkyan War cemetery, near Rangoon, and his Victoria Cross was received by his widow, Ruby, who passed it on to his father, who proudly displayed it in his Finsbury pub. In 1958 it was stolen and its current whereabouts are unknown.

Conclusion

With the defeat of the Japanese in August 1945, the Second World War came to an end. The ensuing years have seen numerous military actions, including wars in Korea, the Falklands and Iraq in which Victoria Crosses were earned and awarded. In the event, so far, none of these have been awarded to a serviceman from Kent but there seems little doubt that someone will ride the White Horse of the county to further glory sometime in the future. The foregoing accounts reveal that the Men of Kent and Kentish Men do not lack courage and, sadly, there appears to be no end to the sort of conflicts in which such valour may be demonstrated. We must be grateful that such men exist.

Bibliography

Arthur, Max, *Symbol of Courage* (London: Sidgwick & Jackson, 2004)

Ashcroft, Michael, *Victoria Cross Heroes* (London: Headline, 2006)

Atkinson, CT, *The Queens' Own Royal West Kent Regiment 1914–1919* (London: Simpkin, Marshall, 1924)

Best, Brian (ed), *The Journal of the Victoria Cross Society* (various issues)

Blaxland, Gregory, *The Buffs* (London: Leo Cooper, 1972)

Brazier, Kevin, *The Complete Victoria Cross* (Barnsley: Pen & Sword, 2010)

Chaplin, HDD, *The Queen's Own Royal West Kent Regiment, 1920–1950* (London: Michael Joseph, 1954)

Clark, EBS and Tillot, AT, *From Kent to Kohima* (London: Gale & Polden, 1951)

Cole, C, *McCudden VC* (London: William Kimber, 1976)

Daily Telegraph, 21 May 1949

Duckers, Peter, *British Gallantry Awards 1855–2000* (Princes Risborough: Shire, 2001)

——, *The Victoria Cross* (Princes Risborough: Shire, 2005)

Franks, N and Saunders, A (2008), *Mannock: The Life and Death of Major Edward Mannock, VC DSO MC RAF* London: Grub Street.

Holt, Tonie and Holt, Valmai, *Battlefield Guide to the Somme* (Barnsley: Pen & Sword, 2006)

Keane, Fergal, *Road of Bones: The Siege of Kohima 1944* (London: Harper Press, 2010)

Kent & Sussex Courier, 14 August, 1914

Perrett, Bryan, *Last Stand: Famous Battles Against the Odds* (London: Arms and Armour Press, 1991)

Slater, Guy (ed), *My Warrior Sons: The Borton Family Diary, 1914–18* (London: Peter Davies, 1973)

Index